On Love, Confession, Surrender and the Moral Self

READING AUGUSTINE

Series Editor:
Miles Hollingworth

Reading Augustine offers personal and close readings of St. Augustine of Hippo from leading philosophers and religious scholars. Its aim is to make clear Augustine's importance to contemporary thought and to present Augustine not only or primarily as a pre-eminent Christian thinker but as a philosophical, spiritual, literary, and intellectual icon of the West.

Volumes in the series:

On Ethics, Politics and Psychology in the Twenty-First Century
John Rist

On Love, Confession, Surrender and the Moral Self
Ian Clausen

On Education, Formation, Citizenship and the Lost Purpose of Learning
Joseph Clair

On Creativity, Liberty, Love and the Beauty of the Law
Todd Breyfogle

On Consumer Culture, Identity, The Church and the Rhetorics of Delight (forthcoming)
Mark Clavier

On Self-Harm, Narcissism, Atonement and the Vulnerable Christ (forthcoming)
David Vincent Meconi

On God, The Soul, Evil and the Rise of Christianity (forthcoming)
John Peter Kenney

On Music, Sound, Affect and Ineffability (forthcoming)
Carol Harrison

On Love, Confession, Surrender and the Moral Self

Ian Clausen

Bloomsbury Academic
An imprint of Bloomsbury Publishing Inc

B L O O M S B U R Y
NEW YORK • LONDON • OXFORD • NEW DELHI • SYDNEY

Bloomsbury Academic
An imprint of Bloomsbury Publishing Inc

1385 Broadway	50 Bedford Square
New York	London
NY 10018	WC1B 3DP
USA	UK

www.bloomsbury.com

BLOOMSBURY and the Diana logo are trademarks of Bloomsbury Publishing Plc

First published 2018

© Ian Clausen, 2018

All rights reserved. No part of this publication may be reproduced or transmitted in any form or by any means, electronic or mechanical, including photocopying, recording, or any information storage or retrieval system, without prior permission in writing from the publishers.

No responsibility for loss caused to any individual or organization acting on or refraining from action as a result of the material in this publication can be accepted by Bloomsbury or the author.

Library of Congress Cataloging-in-Publication Data
Names: Clausen, Ian, author.
Title: On love, confession, surrender and the moral self / Ian Clausen.
Description: New York : Bloomsbury Academic, 2017. | Series: Reading Augustine | Includes bibliographical references and index.
Identifiers: LCCN 2017019302 (print) | LCCN 2017037079 (ebook) | ISBN 9781501314216 (ePub) | ISBN 9781501314223 (ePDF) | ISBN 9781501314193 (hardcover)
Subjects: LCSH: Augustine, of Hippo, Saint, 354-430. Confessiones. | Augustine, of Hippo, Saint, 354-430. | Authorship. | Augustine, of Hippo, Saint, 354-430–Influence. | Love–Moral and ethical aspects.
Classification: LCC BR65.A62 (ebook) | LCC BR65.A62 C535 2017 (print) | DDC 270.2092–dc23
LC record available at https://lccn.loc.gov/2017019302

ISBN:	HB:	978-1-5013-1419-3
	PB:	978-1-5013-1420-9
	ePub:	978-1-5013-1421-6
	ePDF:	978-1-5013-1422-3

Series: Reading Augustine

Cover design: Catherine Wood
Cover image © blackred/Getty Images

Typeset by Integra Software Services Pvt. Ltd.

To find out more about our authors and books visit www.bloomsbury.com. Here you will find extracts, author interviews, details of forthcoming events, and the option to sign up for our newsletters.

To Lauren

CONTENTS

Acknowledgments ix
A Note on Text and Translations xii
List of Abbreviations xiii

Introduction: Being Where We Are   1
   What do we want?   3
   Where are we?   8
   Where are we going?   12

1 Waking Restless Hearts   15
   The (m)othered self, or lovers in need   16
   The rootless self, or lovers in search of home   21
   The seeking self, or lovers of wisdom   25

2 Avoiding the Question   31
   Locating Adam in Genesis 3   32
   Locating Augustine in *Confessions* VIII   38
   Locating Christ in the early works   41

3 Engaging the Despair of Skepticism   47
   Seeking and doubting   49
   Seeking, not finding   55
   Seeking as praying   63

4 Escaping the Folly of Manichaeism   73
   Turning inside out   74
   Turning outside in   85
   Turning inside up   92

5 Entering the Problem of Adam's Place 101
  Starting from faith 102
  Reclaiming the agent 111
  Approaching understanding 118

Conclusion: The Long Surrender 125

References 129
Index 137

ACKNOWLEDGMENTS

I have been reading and writing on Augustine for over nine years, beginning with my first year as a (post)graduate student in Edinburgh. In that time I got married; Lauren and I had our two children, Ainsley and Emma; and we moved seven times across two continents and three institutions. So this book, needless to say, was a journey in itself, teaching us much about patience and grace. In that spirit, I have many people to thank for the journey.

I want to thank two mentors, Oliver O'Donovan and Sara Parvis, who supported this project from its very inception. I owe a special thanks to Oliver O'Donovan for steering me toward Augustine and away from epistemology! This project owes a debt to two funding bodies, the British Marshall Scholarship Commission and the University of Edinburgh Scholarships Office. Many thanks to Robert Lawrie, Mary Denyer, and Elizabeth Clark. I also want to thank the many reviewers of this project who each weighed in at different stages of development: Fergus Kerr, Jane Dawson, Karla Pollmann, John Rist, and Robert Dodaro.

At Edinburgh, my time was spent in the company of many friends. I want to thank especially members of the so-called "Doctrine Group": Tom Miller, Alice Gerth, Phil Reimer, Simon and Marilyn Burton, Sarah Kemlo, Laura Clifton, Josh Coutts, Pippa Gaster, and Jenny Leith. I arrived at Edinburgh having read too much Hauerwas and not enough Augustine; thanks to Joshua Hordern for setting me on the right path. I could not neglect to mention my friendship with Graeme McClelland, who taught me much about Scotland and much more about myself.

At Valparaiso, I had the pleasure of writing this book among those committed to religious education. My thanks to Joe Creech, Director of the Lilly Fellows Program; to Mary Beth Fraser Connolly and Kathy Sutherland, who supported my every step; and to my two mentors, Fred Niedner and Gilbert Meilaender. I am grateful to my fellowship cohort, Katherine Kennedy Steiner (and Joel Steiner) and Michael Cover, and to the students, faculty, and staff at Christ College, especially Slavica Jakelić.

At Villanova, where this book finally came to completion, I began to understand what it means to be a teacher-scholar. I have learned much from Paul Camacho, Matthew Puffer, and Peter Busch, and have thrived under the wise leadership of Marylu Hill and Gregory Hoskins. I also want to thank my Villanova students, particularly members of the Augustine and Culture Seminar Program, whose readings of Augustine have helped to clarify my own. At a critical point, Mary Weatherup stepped in with invaluable input; my thanks to Mary Beth Simmons at the Writing Center for this opportunity. With generous support from the Villanova Veritas Award, I had the necessary support to sharpen and improve this book immensely. Conversations with Catherine Conybeare, Fr. Allan Fitzgerald, OSA, and Jim Wetzel also added to my knowledge and understanding of Augustine.

I want to thank especially my editor, Miles Hollingworth, who never lost sight of what he believed I was capable of; I am truly grateful for your encouragement, as well as the opportunity to represent the *Reading Augustine* series.

To my parents, who never doubted that this day would finally come, and who also often wondered why it was taking me so long, I have few adequate words to express my gratitude, but let me say just a few: your unstinting support for my career path; your love and encouragement; your tireless prayers for me, Lauren, and our family; and your steadfast faith in God's plan for our lives. What I say in this book about God "holding a place for the self," I first experienced through your love and the gift of your presence.

To my siblings, Erica, Andrew, and Alex; to Grandma Marie; and to Lauren's parents and family—also mine in law and faith—I pray the words in this book also ring true to your experience, or at least make some sense! The gift of your love is also one I rejoice over, and I am grateful for the lives that you have each chosen to lead.

Lauren and I met in high school, in a speech class no less, where I lost the debate and, as they say, won the girl; though it took some convincing. Now fifteen years later, with two daughters, Ainsley and Emma, we look back with amused fondness at the journey we have taken. I dedicate this book to you, Lauren, for no one else in my life invites the light that you do. Where you are, God willing, is where I always want to be.

IC
Villanova University

A NOTE ON TEXT AND TRANSLATIONS

For the most part, and where available, I have used translations of Augustine from New City Press, *The Works of Saint Augustine: A Translation for the Twenty-First Century*, series editor John Rotelle, OSA, and Boniface Ramsey (1990–). Unless otherwise noted, all translation references refer to this series. Notable exceptions include my use of Peter King's edition of *Contra Academicos* or *De Academicis*: Augustine (1995), *Against the Academicians and the Teacher*, tr. Peter King, Indianapolis, IN: Hackett; Peter King's edition of *De libero arbitrio*: Augustine (2010), *On Free Choice of the Will, on Grace and Free Choice, and Other Writings*, tr. Peter King, Cambridge: Cambridge University Press (Cambridge Texts in the History of Philosophy); Robert P. Russell's edition of *De ordine*: Augustine (2008 [1948]), *Divine Providence and the Problem of Evil: A Translation of St. Augustine's De Ordine*, tr. Robert P. Russell, OSA, Washington, DC: The Catholic University of America Press (Fathers of the Church Patristic Series); and at one point, Silvano Borruso's translation of *De ordine*: Augustine (2007), *On Order (De Ordine)*, tr. Silvano Borruso, South Bend, IN: St. Augustine's Press. For Augustine's Latin I consulted the *Nuova Biblioteca Agostiniana* (1965–), Roma, Città Nuova Editrice. All biblical quotes, unless drawn from Augustine, are taken from the Revised Standard Version.

LIST OF ABBREVIATIONS

C	*Confessions* (*Confessiones*), tr. Maria Boulding, OSB (2001)
EP	*Expositions of the Psalms* (*Enarrationes in Psalmos*), tr. Maria Boulding, OSB (2000).
FCW	*Free Choice of the Will* (*De Libero Arbitrio*), tr. Peter King, Cambridge: Cambridge University Press (2010).
FU	*Faith in the Unseen* (*De Fide Rerum Invisibilum*), tr. Michael G. Campbell (2005).
GRM	*Genesis: A Refutation of the Manichees* (*De Genesi contra Manichaeos*), tr. Edmund Hill (2002).
HGJ	*Homilies on the Gospel of John* (*In Evangelium Ioannis Tractatus*), tr. Edmund Hill, OP (2009).
L	*Letters* (*Epistula*), tr. Roland Teske, SJ (2001).
OO	*On Order* (*De Ordine*), tr. Robert P. Russell, Washington, DC: The Catholic University of America Press (2008 [1948]); also in one place, tr. Silvano Borruso, Indianapolis, IN: South Bend, IN: St. Augustine's Press (2007).
R	*Revisions* (*Retractationes*), tr. Boniface Ramsey and Roland Teske, SJ (2010).
S	*The Soliloquies* (*Soliloquiorum*), tr. Kim Paffenroth (2000).
TA	*The Academics* (*De Academicis*), tr. Peter King, Indianapolis, IN: Hackett (1995).
TAB	*The Advantage of Believing* (*De Utilitate Credendi*), tr. Ray Kearney (2005).
TC	*Teaching Christianity* (*De Doctrina Christiana*), tr. Edmund Hill, OSA (1996).
TCG	*The City of God* (*De Civitate Dei*), tr. William Babcock (2012).

TCWL/TMWL	*The Catholic Way of Life/The Manichean Way of Life* (*De Moribus Ecclesiae Catholicae et De Moribus Manichaeorum*), tr. Roland Teske, SJ (2006).
THL	*The Happy Life* (*De Beata Vita*), tr. Roland Teske (2010).
TPS	*The Predestination of the Saints* (*De Praedestinatione Sanctorum*), tr. Roland Teske, SJ (2011).
TR	*True Religion* (*De Vera Religione*), tr. Edmund Hill, OP (2005).
TS	*To Simplicianus* (*Ad Simplicianum*), tr. Roland Teske, SJ (2011).
TT	*The Trinity* (*De Trinitate*), tr. Edmund Hill, OP (1991).
TTS	*The Two Souls* (*De Duabus Animabus*), tr. Roland Teske, SJ (2006).

Introduction:
Being Where We Are

This is a book about the animating center of the moral life; how that center is love; and how it is love that makes us restless creatures of migration, introspection, and hope, borne by a motion we do not always understand, heading in a direction we do not fully control; as Augustine famously declared at the end of his *Confessions*, "my weight is my love, and wherever I am carried, it is this weight that carries me" (*C* XIII.9.10).

This is a book about the legacy of Augustine: author of *Confessions,* and many other books. It maps Augustine's journey to confessing love's weight on the way to becoming the famous saint he is today. To be precise, this book examines a short period of writing, the "early works," that unfolds between two key events in Augustine's life: his conversion to faith in AD 386, and his appointment to the priesthood in AD 391. In this period, Augustine raises many questions about love, and many times invites *us* to question love as well. He summons us to an exercise of moral introspection that teaches us to track down the furtive movements of love. In so doing he delivers us to the gift that is love, inviting us to contemplate love's source and destination.

For Augustine, to love is a condition of the self. Loving is what enables us to be, know, and will (*esse, nosse, velle*; *C* XIII.10.11). In this book, our aim is to travel with Augustine as he shows us how to be "where we are" through love. To do this, this book deploys four terms of analysis: love, confession, surrender, and the moral self. If *love* refers to the motion that animates the soul, *confession* refers to the act of acknowledging this motion; *surrender* refers to the posture implicit in that confession; and *the moral self* refers to the place of personal reckoning and conversion—a place that enfolds the other terms into itself. For though each lights up an important aspect of his thought, the moral self draws a line under the fundamental experience that haunts and enchants Augustine's theological-moral vision.

This is the experience of being found in a place, of having to reckon with oneself in encounter with the other. It is the experience of trying hard to give account of the self, only to find the process difficult and relentlessly self-exposing. In a way, it is the story of Augustine in *Confessions*: a story that in many ways is *our* story as well. It is a story, as one scholar puts it, that remains for us today "preeminently the metaphysics of conversion" in the West (Gilson 1960: 240). It is the story that has given us to ourselves and each other, setting off crucial developments in Western history, culture, and politics. What animates this story is a journey of desire that unfolds its destination through a self-disclosing encounter: namely, one with the Creator God himself. This encounter brings forth a decisive self-reckoning that demands personal account of my location in the world: "where I am" as a lover "on the way" [*in via*]. In his ability to speak to us today about this process, Augustine addresses perhaps the hardest thing for any person to do: stand still for a moment, take measure of my "place," and begin truly to reckon with the truth of my position. As we do so through reading Augustine, we confirm the wise adage that "the hardest thing in the world is to be where you are" (Williams 2003: 21, 83).

* * * *

This adage is entertained throughout this book, aiding and illuminating our reading of Augustine. I propose its simplicity conceals a profound insight that Augustine's moral journey can divulge and explore. Not that Augustine's is the only route to take, or that he and he alone defines the truth of "where we are." But rather that he offers us a compelling moral framework that haunts the fractured landscape of the age of modernity.

This claim is in one sense historical fact. Augustine's influence on the West, theologically and otherwise, has been observed and commented on by many prominent scholars (see, most recently, Pollmann 2013). His influence on the development of the Western moral tradition has attracted substantial attention from admirers

(Rist 2014) and critics (Connolly 2002). His relevance to us in any historical sense is outmatched by his enduring ability to captivate the heart. Readers from all backgrounds continue to claim him, and those who disagree with him still call him their friend (Arendt 1996: 115). For them, Augustine is no relic of history but a timelessly suasive reader of the human moral condition. He tells us something about who we are today, and the loss of this something is not something one should take lightly.

Indeed, I want to make a greater claim on his behalf. His legacy in approaching questions of the self—or "moral self"—is like the echo of a voice calling out to us still. It is a monument to what we once were and could be, and may be the truth of who we are in the end. In setting out to re-read Augustine today, we can test the validity of his prayer on our behalf: "For a little while yet there is light for human beings; let them walk in it, yes, let them walk, lest the darkness close over them [John 12:35]" (C X.22.33). Maybe Augustine can tell us where we ought to be heading, or maybe he only shows us why we chose the opposite way. No one who reads him with charity, however, can fail to come away having a sense of the question.

What do we want?

Our first task in this introduction is to specify this "question" for the purpose of addressing its implications for today. What makes this difficult, however, is not just Augustine's antiquity, but the modernity that renders us a question to ourselves.

To be modern on one view is to struggle with location. It is to struggle with not knowing where we are or where we are going. Though this struggle may have origins in diverse modern events—secularization, globalization, modern technology, etc.—altogether, it underwrites and fuel the assumption (if not presumption) that the modern is a condition of being permanently out of place. As Nietzsche once described it, this age is endemically homeless. It hurtles us forward without letting us look back.

> We children of the future, how *could* we be at home in the present? We are unfavorable to all ideals which could make us feel at home in this frail, broken-down, transition period; and as regards the

'realities' thereof, we do not believe in their *endurance*. The ice which still carries us has become very thin: the thawing wind blows; we ourselves, the homeless ones, are an agency that breaks the ice, and the other thin "realities".... (Nietzsche 2006: 192 [377]; translator's emphasis)

Since most do not attain Nietzsche's vision of the *Übermensch*, realizing this state is not a moment of liberation, but rather can be a source of anxiety about existence. And it is not hard to see why. If home is our identity, but this age keeps us homeless, this forces us to labor toward establishing an identity that cannot *be* established without forsaking modernity itself. With the past no longer accessible to the projected modern subject, turning back to past authors even as luminous as Augustine seems like we are living in denial of our condition. What help is to be gained from reading a fourth-century Church Father?

Anxiety over place is nothing new to humanity, but the experience takes on troubling dimensions in modernity. Theories abound on what exactly transpired: one such theory, the so-called "secularization thesis" (largely abandoned by contemporary sociologists), explains our sense of displacement in terms of the decline of religion. It goes something like this:

With the gradual hollowing-out of religious traditions, specifically Western Christianity, a gaping void has opened in the Western self-concept. It is a void that unsettles and threatens modernity, leaving moderns with no choice but to fill it on their own—God has ceased to speak the words "Let there be light" (Gn. 1:2). Instead, nothing prevails where the self once was, forcing self-creation out of the nothing that remains. However, insofar as this nothing *does* prevail, it radically reorients the self in its place. Exposed to the void at the center of existence, the self must decide what it means for itself. If some seize the moment as a golden opportunity, releasing the creativity of human self-expression ("expressive individualism"), others perhaps suffer under the burden it imposes—the burden to self-create—and look around desperately for something more substantial. For the latter, validation is the key to identity, yet they cannot find it within the former religious system. What happens in either case is anyone's guess; but in the moment when this nothingness prevails and confronts us it places us moderns at the edge of a precipice, leaving us to ponder whether to jump or to fly.

As memorialized by W.B. Yeats in "The Second Coming" (1919: 1–3): "Turning and turning in the widening gyre/The falcon cannot hear the falconer;/Things fall apart; the center cannot hold ...."

This secularization thesis rooted in Weberian "disenchantment" is by no means the only story to tell of modernity. Yet it maintains a valid purchase on the modern self-awareness by identifying its evacuation of a dominant religious vision, Western Christianity. Today, as a result of this broken hegemony conflicting voices resound within an increasingly expanding discourse (or discourses). This too is part of what it means to be modern, and the result is a revolution in the self's self-regard. As Kierkegaard once observed, "The times are past when those called poor and insignificant had no conception of themselves ..." (Kierkegaard 2009: 89). For Kierkegaard, this breakthrough was a gift of Christianity, though a gift we have squandered and abused in many ways. Here too a story or genealogy can be told, for according to Larry Siedentop it began with Christianity: specifically, the Christian "invention" of the individual (Siedentop 2014). Ancient peoples viewed themselves on much different terms, as members first and foremost of the family, tribe, and polis. In Christianity, however, they would encounter the radical notion that humans have equality before God despite their station. Over time the seeds of this individualizing vision would sprout the dominant framework of modern self-understanding: political liberalism. What is more, Siedentop assigns an important role to Augustine as the harbinger of today's modern notion of autonomous will (Siedentop 2014: 100–112). Whether or not he is correct on this reading of Augustine (see Chapter 5), he holds an intuition shared by many other scholars, notably Charles Taylor, with regards to the alleged "modernity" of Augustine's many achievements.

For Taylor, it was Augustine's radical notion of reflexivity (or inwardness) that laid the fertile soil for the Cartesian revolution. "In Augustine's doctrine, the intimacy of self-presence is, as it were, hallowed, with immensely far-reaching consequences for the whole of Western culture" (Taylor 1989: 140). Among them was the opening of a new frontier that ushered into existence the modern self-consciousness: an awareness of myself as a self-determining subject, and therefore a subject *I* possess *unto myself*. Not that Augustine would have wanted this to happen, or that he underwrites all the claims made on its behalf; yet for Taylor, we owe this development uniquely to Augustines's famous interior journey set forth in *Confessions*.

At the same time, this radical inwardness has created unique problems that bedevil modern discourse at the deepest of levels (Cary 2000). For example, an insulated and fully self-determining subject—"the self-made self"—has an opaque relation to the "outside," objectified world. In fact, it appears not to occupy a worldly place, but is a free-floating satellite orbiting the world and choosing willy-nilly when and where it touches down. In envisioning this self-made entity called the self, we verge upon Taylor's notion of the modern "buffered self" (Taylor 2007: 38). This self, unmoored from the gravity of the world (creation), is no longer receptive to the call of the falconer (creator). Again, though, if this change is foreboding to some, presaging the decline and dissolution of the self, for others it announces a new day of liberation that opens the frontier to greater individual expression.

What lies at the foundation of this greater self-expression is our sense of increased control over the nature of the self. This perception of control, whether illusory or not, builds on modernity's greater control over nature itself (especially through technology) and the requisite silencing of nature's claim on our condition—for nature cannot tell us what we are anymore (Gilson 2009). Moreover, it is evident this silencing of nature goes together with the silencing of a self-communicating God—for neither can God tell us what we are anymore. If so, then insofar as this perception still claims us, to that extent does it put us arguably *at odds* with Augustine's approach.

Indeed, many scholars who claim this is so (and who dispute Taylor's narrative) tend to observe a radical break between modernity and Augustine (Hanby 2003; Drever 2013). Dramatizing the modern as a decisive moral turn propped up by a decisive metaphysical break with antiquity (or the "pre-modern" age), these scholars counter-claim that the legacy of Augustine, especially his theological and moral legacy, poses a substantive moral challenge to the modern self-conception: that is, by denying that the self is self-made (or buffered) and by affirming an essential "otherness" at the center of the self—the otherness of God (Mathewes 1999). Moreover, these scholars invite readers of Augustine to "retrieve" Augustine's legacy for the sake of the present. They do so by encouraging us to attend to a reality that modernity fails to address or has addressed insufficiently: the reality of love at the center of the Augustinian self.

What, we might ask, does love have to do with the self? In a word, it has everything to do with the self, for without it there is simply no self to consider. Placing love at the center of the question of the self, whatever that may mean, shifts the very ground on which we talk about the self. It moves us from a self made unto itself to a self formed relationally by things (people, places, objects) that it loves. As lovers, and specifically as lovers of the good (see Chapter 1), human beings form a conception of themselves *through* their beloved. This is not to say humans always love rightly, or that they automatically grasp the very *fact* that they love. Rather, it is to suggest that human being, knowing, and willing is inescapably conditioned by the things one desires.

For Augustine, it is precisely reflection on love that activates awareness of the self as a *moral* self. Conversely, it is precisely ignoring love's weight that inhibits an awareness of one's moral and spiritual condition—if not obscures it entirely.

Turning back to our reading of Augustine in this book: if it is easy for all parties in the debate to agree that Augustine "occupies a vexed place in modernity's vexed self-understanding" (Hanby 2003: 6), knowing that vexation for what it is and what it calls for—if it calls for anything—is the more pressing challenge facing readers of Augustine. It is the challenge of not only contending with Augustine but contending with ourselves in what we believe in, hope for and love. The call issuing from Augustine, "Know thyself!," applies to every generation seeking to navigate the world (O'Donovan 2015). If today we find it difficult to hear and to heed, that perhaps says something about the object of our desires.

> We have been modern now for several centuries. We are modern and we want to be modern. We give ourselves an order to be modern. But the fact that the will to be modern has been at work for centuries—carrying us through revolution upon revolution and endless remodeling of the conditions of life—means that we have not yet arrived at being truly modern. We have not yet arrived at being able to say, "here at last is the goal of our undertaking, here at last is the object we grasp." How could we have willed for so long and allowed ourselves to be so often deceived? Is it, perhaps, that we might not know what we truly want? (Manent 2013: 1).

Where are we?

The next step is to interrogate our concept of the moral self. The initial problem in this context is one of translation. Not only did Augustine not have a term for "the self." Inserting that term into his English translation, as many editions do, has confused more than clarified debate about his legacy—so runs an argument by John C. Cavadini (Cavadini 2007).

In fact, for Cavadini the term is misleading. By applying it to Augustine, scholars smuggle in dubious assumptions that leave them chasing shadows of their own self-image. Claiming to have isolated a *thing* called *the self*, scholars assume that they know what that means in Augustine, because they know what that means in our struggle to define it. The problem is, says Cavadini, "once one becomes used to talking about Augustine and 'the self,' it is so much easier for us to argue for retrospective connections between Augustine and any modern theory of 'the self'" (Cavadini 2007: 120). In short, scholars unwittingly conform Saint Augustine to the dominant image of our modern discontent.

And while that image has its notable variations across time, it often reduces down to the following presumption: at the core, human beings are autonomous moral agents, owing their allegiance to no one else but themselves. To be a self, we think, is to determine our identity, exercising full control over who and what we are. Maximal autonomy becomes the goal and ideal, for only then can we claim to be what the age calls "authentic selves," shaped not by anything above or prior to us, as in a law or a god, but only by whatever we have crafted by our will—this "will" being the highest good we value in the world.

Now the origin of this image can be difficult to trace, and very few defend it in its absolute sense. In this case what matters is its imaginative function: how it seems to fulfill many modern assumptions as the logical extension of various half-baked moral claims. The image hovers over us as an inchoate thought, enticing many a modern to give chase and embrace it. Holding forth the possibility of a placeless rootless self, an entity in orbit over and above the traditional groundings (nature, society, culture, God), it presents us with a platform for clearing off the deck, for resetting the (virtual) game, and thereby wresting total control over the ordering of reality (or at least *our* reality, which may amount to the same thing). Puncturing the vacuity of this inflated self-conception is a pastime of many a theologian and philosopher. I indulge in one example from theologian David Bentley Hart:

> We live in an age [the modern age] whose chief moral value has been determined, by overwhelming consensus, to be the absolute liberty of personal volition, the power of each of us to choose what he or she believes, wants, needs, or must possess; our culturally most persuasive models of human freedom are unambiguously voluntarist and, in a rather debased and degraded way, Promethean; the will, we believe, is sovereign because unpremised, free because spontaneous, and this is the highest good. And a society that believes this must, at least implicitly, embrace and subtly advocate a very particular moral metaphysics: the unreality of any "value" higher than choice, or of any transcendent Good ordering desire towards a higher end. Desire is free to propose, seize, accept or reject, want or not want—but not to obey .... And so, at the end of modernity, each of us who is true to the times stands facing not God, or the gods, or the Good beyond beings, but an abyss, over which presides the empty, inviolable authority of the individual will, whose impulses and decisions are their own moral index. (Hart 2003: 47)

Yet, while this is finely said and conveys our basic point, let us not forget the image has its origin in a struggle. It did not arise with such decadence in view but often sprung from a inchoate aspiration to justice; Prometheus, we recall, gave the gift of fire to humans, bestowing blind hopes as well as protection from Zeus. Whether or not its current form as a "debased" Promethean image is the logical extension of such hopes for advancement, the image serves as a useful standard with which to measure modern assumptions against the assumptions that we find in Augustine.

Thus, however noble in its aspiration for justice, the debased image runs afoul of several Augustinian commitments. First, its notion of the self-determined self fails to reckon with the reality conditioning being, knowing, and willing. If love, not will, is the primal reality, and if everything unfolds within the movement of love's weight, then for Augustine it follows not "I am what I will," but more daringly stated "I am what I love"

(Smith 2016). Second, the insularity of the Promethean self-image fails to comprehend the purpose of Augustinian interiority. It is not a closing-off or shutting-out of reality, as Cavadini protests, (see below), but a disciplined self-opening and response to God's call. And third, Augustine's emphasis on "call" and "response" fills the landscape left barren in the modern self-conception. Instead of a self left stranded in an isolated place—or no place at all—the moral self occupies a place through encounter: specifically an encounter with the otherness of God.

In these respects, we follow Cavadini's persuasive insight. "The images that Augustine uses for the content of self-awareness ... are all essentially images trying to describe self-awareness as precisely *not* the awareness of a stable, statue-like entity which may need cleaning or some touch-up polishing, but rather the awareness of a subject in transformation, undergoing transformation, being transformed, re-created ..." (Cavadini 2007: 123). Indeed, they are images pointing readers to a process: a journey, if you like, that does not leave us as we are, but draws us into the presence of the divine transforming life. Cavadini continues:

> The content of self-awareness, for those truly self-aware, is much more disturbing and mysterious, more exciting and hopeful, more treacherous and full of risk. Someone who is self-aware is aware not of "a self" but of a struggle, a brokenness, a gift, a process of healing, a resistance to healing, an emptiness, a reference that impels one not to concentrate on oneself, in the end, but on that to which one's self-awareness propels one, to God. (Cavadini 2007: 123)

In other words, avoid approaching the Augustinian self as if the self were a *thing* that we could observe from a distance. As we are the very "thing" that we seek to observe, our observation includes us as object and subject. There is no glass divider to place in-between us (or "us and us"), for knowledge of the self is not obtained from outside. Tempted as we are by its promise of control, we must learn that "outside" is not a place that we can be. Only God stands outside (but also inside!) and we are not him.

Second, we must learn that to "enter inside" is to strive for awareness of our true, present location. This is what Augustine calls interiority. The self turns into and enters itself—but not *by* itself, *for* itself, *unto* itself, and not from *outside* of its placement in reality. Instead, the self is always taking place within a question: a question at the center of humanity's being, knowing, willing. Hearing this question is the work of the heart, and responding is acknowledging where one is before God. Before revealing this question, I must first reiterate that responding to this question both begins and ends with love. "Love asks; love seeks; love knocks; love reveals; love, finally, remains in what has been revealed" (*TCWL* I.17.31). As the soul's motive energy and interior weight, love is the *means* to a proper self-knowledge, and as the soul's ultimate object and final destination, love is also the *content* and *end* of self-knowledge (Chapter 1, section "The seeking self, or lovers of wisdom"). Love is not only the condition for self-knowledge. It is also the source of much confusion in self-knowledge. It keeps us moving when we want to stand still and keeps us still when we want to start moving. The paradox surfaces in Cavadini's insight that the more we "possess" a true awareness of the self, the more we come to recognize transformation taking place. We are in that sense lovers "on the way" [*in via*] (*EP* 26[2].17) unfinished until the day that we arrive at our destination.

However, there is more we have to say about that journey, for there is also the place that we inhabit right now: the place of the moral self. In this place we encounter responsibilities and obligations, and discover the many relations that constitute our being, knowing, willing. Conversely, by entertaining the modern self-image, the self-made self, we conduct a dangerous experiment in escaping moral reality. Rather than find ourselves inside that reality, we seek to transcend it to gain the advantage: a vantage point *beyond* rather than *on* our condition. The allure of this (false) transcendence is familiar to all, and speaks to the control humans desire in their lives. Orbiting reality as a sovereign buffered self, we detach from others who would claim us in our place—including God. The temptation is as old as humanity's story (Gn. 3) yet shades very close to how we view ourselves today. On that score, Augustine might tell us quite plainly that to occupy a place is not an option to consider; it is always and already a condition of our being.

For Augustine, our existence from conception to death is animated by a question that comes to us from God; a question inviting us to reclaim our place, surrendering our lives in confession, praise, and love. Introducing this question as God's question in Genesis 3, "Where are you?," I propose a new approach to

Augustine's early development. I suggest that this question posits more than just a question, but quietly serves as the ground and condition of true self-knowledge. The God who first called us to be, know, and will is calling us again to re-enter our place. He is summoning us to restoration to his image and likeness through teaching us to acknowledge our dependence on his love (Chapter 2, section "Locating Adam in Genesis 3"). It is the spirit that animates this question, I submit, that echoes across Augustine's early philosophical works. By invoking it here, I am proposing to show how Augustine seeks to prepare us to respond to God's call. In light of this question, when I refer to the moral self, I am not referring to an entity in isolation from others, much less to a power or a faculty of the soul. Rather, I am referring to a condition of self-awareness, restless but hopeful, trembling but secure, whose place has been illumined and challenged by something else: a question inviting lovers to be where they are. If this is the hardest thing for lovers to do, they have no better guide than the author of *Confessions*.

Where are we going?

That said, is not devoting an entire book to the early works merely a detour to the more desirable destination, *Confessions?* For in many ways *Confessions* is the summit of the journey, whereas everything before it tends to lurk beneath its shadow, providing very little in the way of Augustinian profundity. It is true that these works tend to escape scholarly notice, and in comparison with *Confessions* they do indeed fall short. Yet, while their author did recognize their shortcomings (in *Revisions*), he also stood by them as vehicles of instruction (also in *Revisions*). And precisely *because* they are less well known, they offer a unique way into reading Augustine.

The place to begin is with their call to philosophy, a call Augustine delivers in his first published work, *The Academics*: "Wake up! Wake up, I beg you!" (*TA* I.1.3). This call is an invitation to become lovers of wisdom (philosophers). It signals to the reader that this journey is communal: Augustine is not standing on the sideline barking orders, nor is he pronouncing from on high as a Bishop. His open invitation is refreshing and disarming, dispelling the popular image of a cantankerous dogmatist (which Augustine certainly could be!). Instead, he styles himself as a traveler among travelers. He displays a rawer face to his immediate and future audience. Ranging across the terrain of ancient philosophy, theology, ethics, and borrowing and adapting whatever insights he finds, he combines an unflinching impulse for exploring big questions with an almost expectant confidence that truth *will* be found; for the God who calls us to "ask, seek, knock" is the same God who promises "you shall receive, find, enter" (Mt. 7:7–8).

Characterize such confidence as naïve if you must, but Augustine had his reasons for an optimistic outlook. His immaturity at this time is quite evident in places and does not require us to make his excuses. Too often, however, in trying to pin him down, scholars overlook the obvious about him. The man's entire world had turned inside out (and upside down), and it would take him many years to fully grasp what had happened. His struggle to understand what had happened in this period did not leave him in any doubt that something *had* in fact happened. If the truth is elusive even to those that it claims, it is faith that enables him to seek understanding.

When we turn to read Augustine, we must always keep in mind that his thoughts are not packaged for a reader's rapid consumption. To borrow a compelling metaphor from theologian David Tracy (who borrows it from Erich Heller), "understanding some thinkers is like climbing Mont Blanc; understanding other thinkers is like exploring an ancient city like Rome" (Tracy 2008: 263, citing Heller 1965). Ascending Mont Blanc unveils the landscape around it, while exploring an ancient city ("Rome is chaos") leads to endless winding alleys. And yet, there are treasures to be found in those alleys, and their discovery shows us truths of what it means to be human. Among many such treasures that one finds in Augustine, the most precious is inarguably his view on love: not least his loving surrender of the self through confession.

However, he is not just a teacher of this process, even going so far as to deny himself the title; but he is someone who would live it and model it for others, inviting others to enter the same place that he inhabits. In this period, as he begins to gain a handle on his ignorance, the uncertainty does not plunge him into the depths of despair (Chapter 3), propel him to the heights of arrogant reason (Chapter 4), tempt him to deny the fundamental goodness of reality (Chapter 5), and all because his anchor is a deeper confession that does not depend on his personal achievement. Instead, he has embarked on a long spiritual surrender that will form him and challenge him as much as his readers. Having invited the sun of wisdom to pour forth its rays and dispel from him the darkness of his lingering conceits, he uses this time to urge his readers to join him by asking them to ponder the basic questions of existence: "What do you want?" "Where are you?" "Where are you going?" By drawing on methods of dialogue and narrative, not to mention an invention of his own called "soliloquy" (Stock 2010), he labors to place readers in an intimate conversation with the truth lurking within their own being, knowing, willing.

This triad, by the way, which I borrow from *Confessions*, loosely frames what I call the three paths of this book. The first path centers on the question of *knowing* and explores Augustine's engagement with the Academic Skeptics (*The Academics*, TA). The second path centers on the question of *being* and develops Augustine's defense of creation against the Manichees (*True Religion*, TR). The third path centers on the question of *willing* and sketches Augustine's account of human agency and responsibility (*Free Choice of the Will*, FCW).

Of course, each work is a site of contention and has been from the moment Augustine became Augustine of Hippo. Studies are still written on their arguments and history, and many still dispute their coherence and continuity. It is remarkable how diverse the literary landscape has become. The most recent interventions often defend continuity (Harrison 2006; Gerber 2012; Topping 2012) and have revived old debates concerning Augustine's intellectual development (Teske 2007; Dobell 2009). It is important then to clarify what this book does *not* attempt, which is to sort out all the interesting debates on continuity. If that is the price of admission to this period it will all but ensure its obscurity to readers. At the same time, this book is not immune to this debate and does its best to address challenges where relevant. It maintains a modest view of continuity in Augustine— or rather "development and evolution" (Dupont 2008: 75)—and locates that continuity in Augustine's ongoing effort to better place his readers to become where they are, regaining a true sense of their place in God's world. In no way does he utter the last word on the subject, either for his own works or for all of posterity. Instead, his writings give us the opportunity to begin the long journey toward confessing the moral self.

1

Waking Restless Hearts

This chapter sets out to present the moral self as an awakening, restless lover on the way to finding God. It sets out, in short, to explore the human condition by revealing a restless movement of desire at its center: the weight of love. "[M]y weight is my love," Augustine confesses, "and wherever I am carried, it is this weight that carries me."

Though the nature of love admits of many different views, some popular views diverge sharply from Augustine's. For example, some view love as a purely emotional reaction, setting it at odds with the dispassionate reason ("rationalism"). Others view love as a choice one makes as if selecting and investing in an arbitrary object ("voluntarism"). Still others view love as a sentimental affair that is nice if you can get it but is not very common ("romanticism"). Each view captures some element of truth, but none of them quite captures the view of Augustine.

What does he mean by "my weight is my love"? His image seemingly surrenders all control to love, suggesting it not only influences but determines our trajectory. It turns out this suggestion is not far off the mark; the image is not meant to be a flowery metaphor. Instead, it is a statement on the human condition. It means that we are lovers all the time and all the way down. Love is the condition of human being, knowing, and willing. It implies that love is always operating just below the surface: forging new bonds, reinforcing old attachments, claiming us for any number of causes and pursuits. Does this mean love is outside the lover's control, behaving as a kind of physical law of the universe? Not quite; but nor does it ignore love's effects. Instead, confessing love to be the weight that bears us (note the passive voice) the statement nonetheless calls it *our* weight, *our* love (possessive). Indeed, in acknowledging his position in love Augustine poses a basic question to the reader of his works: "where is my love taking me?"

In this question, I recognize my love has gone before me, and that I may not know exactly where it is or where it is going. By resolving to chase down love's location and direction I embark upon a process of re-claiming where I am: this is the place that we call the moral self. As we shall see, Augustine's ventures on this process of discovery tend to work within three interlocking models of self-knowledge: the (m)othered self, rootless self, and seeking self. In each case one discovers and reclaims one's place as a site of personal encounter with the God of all creation.

The (m)othered self, or lovers in need

It is a fundamental axiom of Augustine's anthropology that the human is a lover all the time and all the way down. Love is a condition of human being, knowing, willing. Moreover, this love is always love for the good, for the human cannot help but love the good in some sense. At the same time, love of good does not make us good lovers, nor prevent us committing evil deeds in love's name. Love is also a matter of evaluation and reason. It encompasses both cognitive and affective dimensions (O'Donovan 1980: 29–32). To evaluate the good is to love it, and vice versa, for indeed the good itself is a condition of our being. Put together, we exist in and through love of the good, which encompasses all our activities of knowing and willing.

That said, it is not easy to isolate love, giving it a concise and widely agreed upon meaning. It is more than just emotion, though it certainly includes emotion. It is more than just reason, though it certainly includes reason. And to maximize confusion it takes a wide range of objects: from our love of ice cream to our love of God and neighbor, and every other imaginable relation and attachment (whereas Latin and Greek have multiple words for love, acknowledging the different contexts that love can inhabit, English alas has only the single word "love," which discourages us from thinking very carefully about its meaning).

On the other hand, it is difficult to identify a case in which love is either absent or void of significance. If we resist its reduction to a special kind of relation—a romance, for instance—we can observe it "at work" in many places and situations, including the simplest of interactions and decisions. For example, why do we sit down at the table to eat? Love of food and good company and the need to unwind. These motives are natural, mundane, automatic, yet no less determinative for why we choose to eat. By focusing on a specific case of eating at the table we can begin to uncover motives that are specific to the case. We observe sitting down at *this* table *this* evening a couple who are dedicated to staying together. To know this about them, that they are committed to each other, can provide a fuller account of why they do what they do. Love pops up in the ordinary and incredible, encompassing a wide range of intensities and intentions. But if the temptation on one side is to wax sentimental, idealizing love to the point of absurdity (Hauerwas 1972; May 2011), the far greater temptation, which may amount to the same thing, is to discount and trivialize its real-world significance. Excluding it, therefore, from how we view the world, we run the risk of blotting out humanity's place in the world. How so?

How does love "place" the human being in the world? The experience of being human is the experience of being placed; as one author puts it, "To be at all—to exist in any way—is to be somewhere, and to be somewhere is to be in some kind of place" (Casey 1998: ix; cited in Bartholomew 2011: 4). To be somewhere does not equate to self-knowledge, but it is the precondition for pursuing self-knowledge. Reaching self-knowledge requires taking an extra step, gaining a perspective on our place in the world. To hold such a perspective or first-personal point of view, the "I" (Scruton 2012: 31, 32), defines the uniquely human way of inhabiting a place. This, though, does not mean one *constitutes* one's place—at least alone—but comes to discover it through encountering the other. Self-knowledge depends on acknowledging the other, through whom we slowly come into awareness of our placement. The gift of the other is the place of the self, for the other makes possible the self's realization.

From this perspective, it is evident that the modern self-image—the self-made self, existing unto itself—is not so much a self as a fatal extrapolation, taking its location *in* the other for granted. It denies that the self has been othered into existence, and that it would not *be* without the other as a gift. Augustine examines this location in a memorable way when he narrates his infancy early on in *Confessions*. Exploring the hidden origins of his budding self-awareness he reflects upon the infant's slow emergence in the world. "Little by little I began to notice where I was [*ubi essem*], and I would try to make my wishes known to those who might satisfy them" (C I.6.8). The beginning of the infant's recognition of its place gains ground through expressing its *need* for the other. In the infant's dawning awareness of his place in the world, Augustine finds a useful analogy for his present adult struggles. Just as infants stand helpless in their place before others, so Augustine stands helpless to recall his own infancy. By relying on other people (testimony) and infants (inference) for insight, he can begin to draw a picture of that shrouded period of life. As he does, he realizes that his needs and desires had been met by some "other" who had been there all along: his mother Monica. The self-as-othered is the self-as-mothered, for mothers stand to provide what the infant cannot give itself: a place (Power 1996: 77, 78).

However, this prompts him to reach further back and to ask where he was before encountering his mother. Who can account for his prior existence? Neither testimony nor inference can help him with that, his whereabouts at that point remaining shrouded in mystery. "Where could a living creature like this have come from, if not from you, Lord? Are any of us skillful enough to fashion ourselves?" (C I.6.10). By drawing an analogy with the mother–infant encounter, he can begin to cry out to the Mother of all: "Tell me, I beg you, tell your miserable suppliant, O merciful God, whether my infancy was a sequel to some earlier age now dead and gone ... Was I somewhere else? Was I even someone? I have nobody to tell me ..." (C 1.6.9; cf. O'Connell 1996, 38, 39). As the infant cries out to its mother for milk, so Augustine cries out to his God for understanding. Even here, in the mysteries of the origin of the soul (a question never settled by Augustine), God's Otherness and "Motherness" holds a place for the self.

By locating the self through the other and mother Augustine challenges modern notions of the place of humanity. If we need other people to secure us a place—if we need other people to exist full stop—then our place is not secured by an autonomous act of will, any more than our identity is defined on its own. In the case of the infant this is obviously true, but less so, perhaps, of the self-possessed adult. However, Augustine argues that human vulnerability is a perpetual condition of the human qua creature. The reason this condition escapes our awareness is partly due to the complexity of mature adult relationships, and partly due to our tendency to take others for granted: not confessing the role that others play in our lives. In general, it can be difficult to recognize oneself as dependent on others who surround and precede it. If "everything is connected," this is not self-evident, nor indeed is it (always) obvious what it demands or requires.

To explore this, Augustine returns to his condition as an infant. "And if I was even conceived in iniquity, and with sin my mother nourished me in her womb [Ps. 50:7], where, I beg of you, my God, where was I, your servant, ever innocent? Where, Lord, and when?" (C I.7.12). Strange as it seems to hold an infant to account, his goal is to shore up his position before God by *taking responsibility* for his response to God's call. In this case, though his infancy remains to him a mystery and eludes his ability to give an account, his attempt nevertheless reminds us that our life is not our own, but unfolds before the others and the Other who have claimed us.

Our location is not only obscure circumstantially. It can also be obscured through a willful self-deceit. To the extent that it commands us to act or to attend; to the extent that it calls us to responsible self-questioning; then the opportunity to ignore it or evade it entirely is a prospect typically seized without question by humans. This is evident most of all in the God–self relation, which serves as the template for Augustine's moral reflections. In *Confessions* book I, drawing on the Parable of the Prodigal Son (Lk. 15), he likens himself to the son who went astray, squandering his inheritance as the father looked on. Observing God's "silence" during his turbulent youth, he wonders at the reasons for God's leniency and forbearance: "How hidden you are, dwelling on high in your silence [Isa. 33:5] ...!" (C I.18.29). In book III, he returns to this theme of God's silence and starts to probe God's location in relation to himself. "Where were you at that time, how far from me?" To which he adds, "I was certainly roving far away from you, and debarred even from the pods I was feeding to pigs" (C III.6.11). Who was the distant one, God or Augustine? By calling into question not God's love but his, Augustine uncovers the hidden truth behind his creaturely displacement: "I was seeking you, my God, not through that power of the mind by which you have chosen to rank me above the beasts, but only through carnal inclination ... [While y]ou were more intimately present to me than my innermost being, and higher than the highest peak of my soul" (C III.6.11).

This statement, one of the most celebrated lines of *Confessions*, offers a model for how to think about the self in its place. Experiencing God's absence is here re-interpreted as indicating a prior moral displacement of the self. It is the self, not God, who willfully stands apart. In wandering from God Augustine strayed from himself; and in allowing him to stray God had stayed where he is, "holding in place" the only place Augustine could be: in God's presence (Marion 2012: 238). If to claim that place is to enter God's presence, to enter God's presence necessarily begins with confession: "you were more intimately present to me than my innermost being ...."

Pressing further, it is clear that God holds us in place not just as God of Creation, the condition of the possibility of creation; but also as the self-communicating God of revelation, a Being who calls us and invites us to himself. Insights on the latter can be drawn from *Confessions*. Primarily, God communicates by the gift of Holy Scripture, the "other" that reveals God's work on our behalf. One reason Scripture floods the narrative in *Confessions* is that its author wants Scripture to claim control of his story; he wants it to show him where he is and where he is going. In seeking authorization from God for his story, he pursues his *Confessions* as something other than (mere) autobiography. If it is such a thing, it is not straightforwardly so, for its author wishes to give up his authorial "rights" to acknowledge the one Author who has held him in place.

Moreover, within the story our author tells about himself, he acknowledges multiple witnesses who helped him along the way. Even in the opening lines of his *Confessions*, the role of the witness is made plain in the general case, when he asks of God, "which comes first: to call upon you or to praise you?" (C I.1.1) This he will resolve by an appeal to Romans 10:14, determining that one calls upon hearing God's word. "[F]or to us you have indeed been preached. My faith calls upon you, Lord, this faith which is your gift to me, which you have breathed into me through the humanity of your Son and the ministry of your preacher" (C I.1.1). In book III, he returns once again to his mother, confessing her role as a witness to the faith. He recalls her dream in which an angel had approached her, declaring "where she stood, there also stood I" (C III.11.19). Monica once more held a place for her son. Her prayers were God's words conveyed directly to him (C II.3.7). In the place of Augustine Monica stood her ground, even evoking the admiration of the Bishop of Milan: "it is inconceivable that he should perish, a son of tears like yours" (C III.12.21). What Augustine above all wants to show in this passage is how thoroughly his position is a gift from the other, a gift that testifies to the faithfulness of God.

Monica was not alone in witnessing to Augustine. The entire created world bore witness to God and would beckon him forth to investigate its goodness. It took him some time to discover *the* good, though, on account of his allegiance to the Manichean sect. Inspired to write his first book "On the Beautiful and the Fitting," now lost, he devoted time to studying the "beautiful things below me ..." (C IV.13.20). Although this book marked a beginning in his quest for the truth, it would also witness against him as a misguided attempt. Heavy desires lay waste to his endeavors of comprehension. "I was thinking about the beautiful and the harmonious, and longing to stand and hear you, that my joy might be perfect at the sound of the Bridegroom's voice [Jn. 3:29], but I could not, because I was carried off outside myself by the clamor of my errors, and I fell low, dragged down by the weight of my pride" (C IV.15.27).

At the same time, his desire for beauty would persist and cause further questions to "well ... up in my mind from my innermost heart" (C IV.13.20). Down at that level, the level of desire and love, God was still lingering in the place of Augustine. The more he learned to stand in that place in stillness, the closer he came to finding the truth of his desire. In the end, he would learn to come down from his pride just as God had come down to show the way of true love. "Life has come down to you, and are you reluctant to ascend and live? But what room is there for you to ascend, you with your high-flown ways and lofty talk? Come down, that you may ascend, ascend even to God, for you have fallen in your attempts to ascend in defiance of God" (C IV.12.18). As we shall see, this advice echoes across Augustine's writings.

The rootless self, or lovers in search of home

"Out of love for loving you do I do this [act of recollection]" (C II.1.1). So Augustine reveals his true motive for confessing. It unfolds within the horizon of his love for the divine, itself a response to God's love in creation. His confession is a performance of the event he longs to enjoy: an intimate conversation and encounter with the truth. As he gathers up his longings for the good, the true, the beautiful, he finds himself heavy with the desire for salvation: "Say to my soul, *I am your salvation* [Ps. 34:3]" (*C* I.5.5) is his constant refrain. His confession serves to build up this longing even more by disclosing God's presence throughout his past wandering journey. One such disclosure occurs in *Confessions* book IV.

Recollecting a period of intense grief in book IV, Augustine unveils the hidden anchors of his wandering restless heart. Ultimately, his answer to the question of desire, "what do we want?," circles around the human need for a place to call a home: for "home" is a place unlike any other place, and cannot be treated as just a project among many. Instead, home constitutes a need of the soul (in Simone Weil's sense). Endemic as an object of human desire, home is at the root of all joys, troubles, and strife. Everything we struggle to attain and defend has a notion of home somewhere lurking in the background. Even its absence gives substance to our being. If not at home or on the way to it, we are probably running from it or trying to find it somewhere else. Synonymous in some sense with happiness itself, "home is where the heart is" in reality and in hope. As often happens, Augustine's experience of losing such a home ultimately revealed the true depth of its significance to his life. Let us explain.

In book IV, Augustine relates the tragic death of his childhood friend, an unnamed companion he had cherished very dearly. In a way, this event marks a moment of decisive clarity, but not before he suffers the excruciating pain of separation. The process is vividly described by the philosopher Simone Weil: "But there is an unspeakable wrench in the soul at the separation of a desire from its object" (Weil 2003 [1947]: 23). For Weil, this pain is part of a process of purification. It illuminates the truth of our position in the world. In book IV, Augustine undergoes a similar process which renders him at once more transparent and opaque. The loss of his friend means his "home" is taken from him, forcing his retraction of desire from the world. This desire now stripped of its intended worldly object, it presses down upon Augustine with the weight of indeterminacy. It needs to have an object, it demands to be placed, but the object it seeks is no longer there on the horizon. Scanning this horizon for his friend now gone, Augustine sinks into a loneliness and darkness overnight. "Black grief closed over my heart and whenever I looked I saw only death. My native land was a torment to me and my father's house unbelievable misery. Everything I had shared with my friend turned into hideous anguish within me" (C IV.4.9). That friend *was* home, and now home is not the same. Death demolished the home that gave Augustine to himself. There opens then a rift between Augustine and himself, unleashing piercing questions that will challenge his position. "I had become a great enigma to myself," he famously writes, "and I questioned my soul, demanding why it was sorrowful and why it so disquieted me, but it had no answer" (C IV.5.9). Indeed, he cannot stand in his place anymore, if even one can call it a place anymore. Trying to lodge hope in a false view of God, hope "would slip through that insubstantial thing and fall back again on me, who had remained to myself an unhappy place where I could not live, but from which I could not escape. Whither could my heart flee to escape itself? Where could I go and leave myself behind? Was there any place of refuge where I would not be followed by my own self?" (C IV.7.12). His loss makes him face the haunting truth of who he is: a lover still in need of a place to call home; and a mortal destined to suffer the same fate as his friend.

This tragic experience also marks a pivot point at which Augustine comes to realize his place in the world. It begins to raise questions that were there all along, and extend beyond Augustine to touch our own lives as well. Do we not face the same experience of loss? And how do we account for the desires it reveals?

Home is the object of desire for Augustine, and the loss of home evokes in him a visceral response. Such a source of security and identity and belonging unleashes powerful emotions when threatened or destroyed (C IV.6.11). What it gives as a basis for declaring who he is it demands as a sacrifice by the giving of himself. As a consequence, Augustine becomes very hard on himself for not loving this friend the way he ought to be loved: as a human (C IV.7.12). His self-criticism can evoke a powerful response within readers, and many of them question his remorse over his grief. His protestations ring hollow and strike the reader as subhuman, for surely it is right for us to grieve the loss of loved ones. Not discounting that Augustine may be wrong about his grief, the first question to ask is how he thinks about his love. In this case, as in so many cases with Augustine, his view of love's nature stands in tension with our own.

To explore this, we turn from Augustine's *Confessions* to a recent philosophical account of the nature of love. In his recent book *Love: A History* (2011), the philosopher Simon May wants to convince his modern readers that their view is mistaken: love is not the thing moderns claim it to be. The modern view of love is instead a devilish fiction, a surreptitious evasion of the human moral condition. Exposing the absurdity of the modern view of love takes May back to consider the origins of modernity itself. He focuses on the presumption of a modern secular age, an age which he claims is far less secular than it proclaims. How is the modern age still religious to the core?

Over a century ago, Friedrich Nietzsche famously proclaimed the death of God while decrying the fact that history (at least 2,000 years of it) had failed to produce another. "But he was wrong," May intervenes in the book's first pages. "That new god was there—indeed was right under his nose. That God was love. Human love" (May 2011: 1). This occurred because moderns, though ostensibly rejecting God, continued to believe God's presence persisted in the world. They continued to believe, not that "God is love," but that "love is God" in the human love-relation (May 2011: 1; citing Singer 1984–87: 294). By inverting *without replacing* the Christian view of love, moderns shackled human love to a set of divine attributes. True love now looked rather curiously familiar: *unconditional*, *disinterested*, *impartial*, *universal*, and *perfect* in every way that once distinguished the Christian God (May 2011: 2). Not only is this problematic from a metaphysical perspective, it also challenges the very notion and possibility of *human* love.

By treating human love as divine in this way, moderns wipe out the features that define human relations. They forget that humans occupy a place in the world, unlike God; and that this place carries with it many conditions and limitations, also unlike God. By mistaking human place as an impediment to love—rather than the condition for expressing human love—moderns foolishly hold love to an impossible standard, one that removes both love *and* humanity from the world (cf. Nussbaum 1990: 365–391). Such a standard is a recipe for despair, May warns, not to mention incoherent as a philosophical position.

For May, any attempt to define human love must arise out of the conditions and needs of the soul. It must begin with things human, not things essentially divine, which means it must be grounded in the human vulnerability. A new definition of love is set forth. "Love, I will argue, is the rapture we feel for people and things that inspire in us the hope of an indestructible grounding for our life. It is a rapture that sets us off on—and sustains—the long search for a secure relationship between our being and theirs" (May 2011: 6). On this account, love is vulnerable and unsteady in its motion. It is yearning for, extending toward, an encounter with the Real, whatever that may be. To return for a moment to Augustine in book IV: it is as if the death of his friend pulled Augustine at the roots, severing his connection to the nourishing soil of friendship. Death revealed him as a vulnerable self, who not only wanted a home but also needed one to survive. What May calls the "desire for ontological rootedness" (May 2011: 6) Augustine identifies as the condition of the created human self. Even when concealed from our self-understanding this desire is always working both on us and in us. More than that, it lays claim to our being, knowing, willing, demanding we direct them to an object that can satisfy, even if temporarily. In this case, the lesson Augustine learns in book IV is that love does not remain in an idle position; it does not stand still in the course of existence. "Every kind of love has its own energy, and in the soul of a lover love cannot be idle; it must lead somewhere. Do you want to discern the character of a person's love? Notice where it leads" (*EP* 121.1). His story in this sense sounds a cautionary note: that love *will* lay down its roots *somewhere*, and is doing so already in the way that we live. Hence, he offers this pithy advice: "Love as much as you like, but take care what you love" (*EP* 31[2].5).

The seeking self, or lovers of wisdom

May's aim is to remind us that love is not divine, or at least it isn't *unambiguously* good at every turn. It can cause us to do extraordinary things in its name, awesome feats that adorn the lengthy halls of human accomplishment. It can also compel us to commit awful deeds while pursuing the same objects that inspire awesome feats. Love's ambiguity is what we often forget—and sometimes *want* to forget for the sake of consolation. In the absence of God we sought security in something else, investing that object with our hopes for the future. The divine love-standard serves to hold us in place — yet at the price of demanding that we transcend our place denying the very possibility of love in the process. Once, we were dismayed by God's non-existence. Now we must be let down by humanity's inevitable lovelessness. The malaise of modernity indeed!

For May, our current idolization of love makes us blind to the treacheries that proceed in love's name. Our anodyne descriptions of the human condition have only left a gaping hole in our self-understanding, pushing us on the one hand to ignore our desires, and on the other hand to pretend to the level of the angels (Nussbaum 1990). The pretense only invites us to screen out realities that confront our condition and invite introspection. In Augustine's case, that reality was the mortality of his friend, which in turn carried the truth of his condition in the world. If we do not want to face such realities at all, then at least let us be honest that our problem is not with God (at least not initially), but simply with the fact that we are human, all too human.

"If we all have a need for love," reasons May, "it is because we all need to feel at home in the world." These needs generate longings that lead to unrest; and restlessness is one thing Augustine knows well. He is, after all, famous for saying, "our heart is unquiet [restless] until it rests in you." But let us quote fully the lines all around this, lines often ignored by the admirer of Augustine. "Yet these humans, due part of your creation as they are, still do long to praise you. You stir us so that praising you may bring us joy, because you have made us and drawn us to yourself, and our heart is unquiet until it rests in you" (C I.1.1). If modern readers tend to resonate with Augustine's last clause, the rest of his statement does not command the same applause. By taking May's ontological rootedness much further, the statement presses love in a decidedly theological direction. First, it bestows a prior meaning on love. More than just a sign of our insecure existence, more than just a vulnerability inherited from birth, restlessness bespeaks to us a tale of redemption that encompasses not only ourselves but the cosmos as well. It tells us that humans have been claimed for something else; that behind our present longings is a God who "stirs" the soul. If May offered a history of what love has become, here Augustine does not hesitate to tell us what it means. And, if we think he is speaking only of himself, we have yet to understand what he is up to in *Confessions*.

For example, in book XI he writes: "I do [confession] to arouse my own loving devotion toward you, and that of my readers, so that together we may declare, *Great is the Lord, and exceedingly worthy of praise* [Ps. 47:2; 95:5; 144:3]." Citing the same verse he invoked in book I, he reveals his intention is to have us confess it; to carry us to a place of confession and love, the place of the moral self, in which this verse comes to claim us as the cry of our soul. Similarly, his statement "our heart is unquiet" is not just a claim but inviting us to claim it. Indeed, it is an invitation to *become* restless hearts, even if it assumes we already *are* restless hearts. By reading *Confessions* in this invitational spirit readers uncover its true goal of communion with the divine. And by reading the early works in this invitational spirit, readers likewise uncover Augustine's fundamental objective, namely, preparation for receiving divine wisdom.

Indeed, Augustine's early call to become true philosophers is really an invitation to become lovers of wisdom. That is what *philosophia* means, after all, as Augustine never tires of recalling to mind (*TA* II.3.7, *OO* I.11.32, *TCWL* I.21.38, *C* III.4.8; cf. Holte 1962: 104ff). Those who debate Augustine's status as a philosopher often fail to recognize his emphasis on love. He would not recognize a distinction between "philosophy" and "theology" (Rist 1994: 5), and would balk at treating the latter as irrational or faith based. For him, philosophy is animated by love (weighty love); or, it is nothing but shooting the breeze. From the moment we heed the call to "ask, seek, knock," to the moment we embrace the promise to "receive, find, enter" (Mt. 7:7–8), love is at the helm driving us forward toward wisdom — which everyone knows comprises "knowledge of human and divine matters" (*TA* I.6.16; cf. Cicero, *Tusculanae Disputationes* IV.26.57 and *De Officiis* II.2.5). Let us break down how this love drives philosophy.

Philosophy begins with the awakening of desire (*TA* I.1.3), embarking on a journey to the object of desire. "This is a journey which is made not by any geographical location on earth, but by the desires of our minds [*affectibus animorum*]" (*EP* 5.11; Burnaby 1939: 93–100). After that, philosophy's next task is to discipline desire, conforming human lovers to an appropriate "way of life" (Hadot 2009; Harding 2008; Nussbaum 2009; Boone 2016). "The foot of the soul is properly understood as love. When it is misshapen it is called concupiscence or lust; when it is well formed it is called love or charity" (*EP* 9.15). Finally, since love is both the means and the end, philosophy's final task is to deliver the soul to enjoyment. "Love moves a thing in the direction towards which it tends. But the dwelling-place of the soul is not in any physical space which the form of the body occupies, but in delight [*delectatione*], where it rejoices to have arrived through love [*per amorem*]" (*EP* 9.15; Cf. Burnaby 1939: 109). Philosophy is, simply put, the pursuit of delight; and if it does not lead there, then we're doing it wrong.

Moreover, Augustine's understanding of the *love* of wisdom, is that this love is response *to* the call of *Wisdom Herself* (O'Connell 1996: 38, 39). "Does not wisdom call, does not understanding raise her voice?" (Prov. 8:1). Which means that philosophy is much more than a discipline; it is also an encounter with the One who is calling. "Philosophy promises that it will display the true and hidden God, and now and again deigns to show us a glimpse of Him through the bright clouds, as it were" (*TA* 1.1.3). In that sense, it is evident that Augustine's philosophy entertains different assumptions than its contemporary namesake.

For Augustine, to embark upon the life of the philosopher is to take responsibility for the love we already possess. Beginning with an idle curiosity and interest, an affinity for problem-solving, or an itch for discovery, our desire grows and grows step-by-step through the process to encompass *all* the loves that we pursue and inhabit. If we falter in our steps or fail to persevere, and allow various distractions to deter and dissuade us, this shows us not so much that we desire no wisdom, but that our love for other things is much stronger than we thought.

Of the many potential obstacles confronting lovers of wisdom, Augustine will identify four especially prominent ones:

> This [avoidance of philosophy] is due to either (*a*) the many different upheavals of this life; (*b*) some thickness or laziness or sluggishness of our dulled minds; (*c*) our despair at finding [wisdom], since the star of wisdom doesn't appear to our minds as easily as the light does to our eyes; or (*d*) the common error that men, having found a false opinion, do not search diligently for the truth if they search at all, and even turn away from the desire for searching. (*TA* II.1.1; translator's emphasis)

The last two obstacles have specific points of reference addressed in Chapters 3 and 4 of this book. For now, we observe that all of these obstacles have little at all to do with one's intellectual abilities. Instead, each originates in a set of desires inhibiting and distracting one's pursuit of the truth, even "turn[ing] [us] away from the desire for searching." Indeed, the great challenge facing Augustine's early readers is the tendency to give up on philosophy altogether. Invoking Jesus' command to "ask, seek, knock" (Mt. 7:7), Augustine strives to bring the reader to a point of decision: "Where are you?"

By contrast, modern philosophy, at least in certain guises, is often accused of failing to entertain love at all. Philosophers today, as judged by a prominent practitioner, have all but "forsaken love, dismissed it without a concept and finally thrown it to the dark and worried margins of their insufficient reason ..." (Marion 2007: 1). Crack open a book in the field of analytic philosophy (or, indeed, analytic theology), and one may be forgiven for not feeling very invited. For Augustinian philosophers, of which perhaps there may be two, the field of modern philosophy appears a vast and expanding wasteland (Rist 2014). Love is hardly mentioned, wisdom is on hold, and philosophers have little to say concerning the major "Life Questions" (Gregory 2012). Then again, to the extent that those questions are endemic; to the extent that, once asked, those questions cannot be unasked (MacIntyre 2006: 196); to that extent does Augustine still haunt the contemporary landscape, more than just the shadow of its intellectual history.

2

Avoiding the Question

Embarking on his Christian philosophical career, Augustine taps the hidden potential and promise of love's weight. He thinks that to locate his readers "in" this weight is enough to spark their interest in its source and destination: what is this love, where is it taking me, and why?

In Chapter 1, I unearthed the roots of this process by unfolding different dimensions of Augustinian self-knowledge. Although each of these dimensions increasingly informs Augustine's thought, the most prominent and important one is his notion of the seeking self. By impressing on his readers Christ's command to "ask, seek, knock" (Mt. 7:7–8) Augustine endeavors to draw his readers into the presence and promise of God: "you shall receive, you shall find, the door shall be opened to you." Yet, once embarking on this journey of desire readers encounter many roadblocks that impede their advancement. In this chapter, we focus on one specific roadblock that lurks at the center of the human moral condition: the sin of human pride (*superbia*). Drawing on Augustine's early account of Genesis 3, I examine pride's distortion of the landscape of reality by displacing human being from the order of creation, "the way things are" [*ordo rerum*].

Genesis 3 brings to the fore the question of displacement by depicting God's encounter with Adam and Eve through a question: "Where are you?" (Gn. 3:9). In this question, I suggest, lies the mystery of existence, not to mention our key to unlocking Augustine's early writings. It allows us to map not only his development but also his own journey to his "place" in a Milanese garden; that is, in *Confessions* book VIII. After showing how this journey involves the re-entering of conscience (*conscientia*)

I sketch a working framework for approaching his early works. I propose that in these works Augustine steadily progresses toward a more precise account of humanity's location: namely, as lovers who depend on God's grace.

Locating Adam in Genesis 3

"The hardest thing in the world is to be where we are." All good maxims have the ability to bend, and this one bends to illumine the moral landscape. Taken too literally it is patently nonsense: where else would we be if not where we already are? Yet, just as identity is not reducible to existence, so location is not reducible to a geographical point: at least not for humans. Instead, for humans and specifically for lovers, location is what we are, what we know, what we will, not to mention what surrounds us, confronts us, escapes us. Our location in that sense is hardly centered upon us, but includes whatever it is that happens to situate our place (e.g., "the other"). Even then, we will struggle to comprehend where that is, so easily are we drawn hither and thither by our loves. Desiring something present but unattainable in the moment, wanting something absent yet present to the heart, pining for former days or anticipating the future, or chasing stray thoughts as they float across the mind ... with tendencies such as these taking us places other than "here," small wonder if we find it hard to be where we are.

If we find our place difficult, it is even more difficult when confronted by moral claims on our attention and behavior. From the claim my daughter has on my attention right now to the claim this stranger has who needs my assistance, it is by far the easier route to respond with indifference, and if forced to it, give excuses to rationalize my behavior. The temptation in moral terms is to deflect responsibility, avoiding any response that would admit an obligation. Do not move a muscle, and maybe it will go away; if not, at the ready is an arsenal of responses I have honed over a lifetime of successful evasion. My "encounter" turns into a confrontation with reality, which often results in my victory and minimal disturbance. But if anyone should disturb and unsettle my place ... well, it could turn into my moment of salvation.

* * * *

In the meantime, persisting in our pattern of evasion we avoid the single question at the center of existence. In his first biblical commentary *Genesis: A Refutation of the Manichees* (AD 388–9), Augustine probes the reason why we evade our location. For him, it is an extension of our displaced condition occasioned and perpetuated by the sin of human pride: the pride that claims lordship over reality itself. By tracking the various steps to this pride in Genesis 3, he unfolds the complex ways that we defy the Creator. Let us explore this.

Starting with the initial act of disobeying God, partaking of the fruit God forbade humans to eat, Augustine traces the root of pride to the serpent's seduction which he says exploits a motive buried deep in the human heart: the desire to be like god (Gn. 3:7). Then, noting a third and, in his view, decisive step, he focuses on the aftermath of the exchange between Adam and God. It begins with God interrogating Adam and Eve, "Where are you?" (Gn. 3:9), and ends with God dismissing Adam and Eve from the Garden (Gn. 3:23). What happens in between is not a simple act of punishment, but an outworking of consequences from the sin of human pride.

When God enters Eden "in the cool of the day" (Gn. 3:8) to walk with the creatures he made in his image, it turns out Adam and Eve are nowhere to be found; they have hidden from each other out of shame for their nakedness. Now trembling in fear in response to God's presence, they anticipate the judgment they assume now awaits them. Instead, the first thing God does is ask a question: "Where are you?," his words taking the appearance of an unknowing utterance. This serves to amplify the tension in the story; and to sharpen the point, Augustine clarifies the question is not intended to show God's surprise at the situation. To think so is to miss the main point of the question, and in fact it is to invite the very judgment the questioner enacts. God's question "Where are you?" is not confessing God's ignorance; it is extending God's invitation for Adam to confess. Presupposing the displacement of Adam and Eve, God exposes any reader who would ridicule his question (i.e. the Manichees) as equally displaced from any claim to the truth. "Adam is now questioned by God," Augustine comments, "not because God doesn't know where he is, but in order to oblige him to confess his sin" (*GRM* II.16.24). In Augustine's view, the passage serves to fulfill the double function of both narrating and testing the location of its readers.

Closely considered, this judgment on the reader's response—Augustine is thinking of the Manichees—implies a set of conditions for correctly engaging Scripture. It matters not only what one knows *about* Scripture, but also *where one stands* in attempting to interpret it (Cameron 2012: 239–250). These conditions for interpreting the truth of the Scriptures trace back to Augustine's earlier efforts at reading. In *Confessions* book III, he will recall his lack of humility when approaching the Bible as a young budding philosopher. "At that time ... I was in no state to enter, nor prepared to bow my head and accommodate myself to its ways" (*C* III.5.9). It matters where one stands, not as just a preliminary measure, giving the benefit of the doubt, but as a disciplined receptivity, enduring patience, and earnest longing; in a word, it requires the Christian virtues of faith, hope, and love (cf. *CT*). In the above case, by declaring the Manichees "impious" for taking God's question as a betrayal of ignorance, Augustine exposes not only the corruption of the Manichees' religion, but likewise the deficiency of their desire to know the truth. "If the Manichees were willing to discuss the hidden meanings of these words in a spirit of reverent inquiry rather than that of captious fault-finding, then they would of course not be Manichees, but as they knocked it would be given them, and as they sought they would find, as they knocked it would be opened to them" (*GRM* II.2.3; paraphrasing Mt. 7:7).

Not only do the Manichees obscure God's question, refusing to receive it "in a spirit of reverent inquiry." By their ridicule they attack the source of salvation—the condition for its possibility—in a manner that mirrors Adam's error in Genesis 3.

Upon receiving God's question Adam indicts his very self. He "answered [God] that when he heard [God's] voice he hid himself, since he was named. His very answer was already an instance of a truly miserable error—as though his being naked, as God himself has made him, could displease God!" (*GRM* II.16.24). To this, Augustine adds that Adam's "truly miserable error" was to think that "what was displeasing to oneself also displeases God." It was an error he could have avoided had he stayed "naked of pretense, but clothed with divine light," as God had originally made Adam and Eve by nature. Yet, since Adam "turned away from [the divine light] and turned to himself ... and was displeased with himself as not having anything he could call his very own" (*GRM* II.16.24), God raised the very question that would spotlight Adam's sin,

"Where are you?," revealing his displacement in relation to the truth. However, instead of accepting God's call to confess, Adam plunged himself more deeply into the abyss of human pride.

Invited yet a second time to clarify events (Gn. 3:11) Adam offers the fateful response, "The woman whom thou gavest to be with me, she gave me the fruit of the tree and I ate" (Gn. 3:12). For Augustine, these words condemn Adam in his place. They show that he occupies not the place of confession, but a dangerous suspension over "the way things are." Augustine comments that this verse shows Adam blaming not only Eve, but also the one who gave the gift of Eve and all good things, namely God. Even worse than blaming Eve, and even worse than disobeying God (*TCG* XIV.14), Adam commits the blasphemous error of *accusing God, the creator, of sin*. This more than anything reveals Adam's pride, in turn widening the (moral) gap between Adam and his Creator. Augustine comments:

> Next, as is the way with pride, [Adam] doesn't plead guilty to being the woman's accomplice, but instead puts all the blame for his own fault on the woman; and in this way, with a subtlety seeming to spring from the cunning the poor wretch had conceived, he wanted to lay his sinning at the door of God himself. He didn't just say, you see, "The woman gave it to me," but more fully: *The woman whom you gave to me.* (*GRM* II.17.25)

Thus, the culmination of Adam's defiance is a claim against God as the author of creation. Installing the human creature in the place of the creator Adam inverts the natural order that defines their relation. In so doing, however, he alone suffers displacement, for God is not a ruler/author in the conventional sense. He does not stand above us as a powerful lord, but is the condition for the possibility of existence itself. Consequently, in attempting to claim God's rule Adam rejects the very condition for his own restoration. By rejecting God's invitation to acknowledge his sin, he walls himself off from the only possible forgiveness; for a sinful God is not a God who can forgive.

On that point, Augustine blasts the Manichean sect for repeating Adam's error through pernicious religious teaching, namely "that the soul is by nature what God is" (*GRM* II.25.38). His judgment is repeated at the end of the text as he clarifies the crux of their dispute on religion:

> *the* religious question is how to think about God in a godly way. Now since we cannot deny that the human race is sunk in the story state of sin, *they* [Manichees] say that God's nature is sunk in a story state, while *we* deny that, and say that the nature which God made out of nothing is sunk in a sorry state, and has come to this pass, not by being forced into it but through its will [*voluntate*] to sin. (*GRM* II.29.43)

Although we take up the question of the will in Chapter 5, let us here note its function in relation to Genesis 3: to erect a secure buttress against Adam's fateful error, accusing God of sin. Thus, Augustine identifies a place we all inhabit—the place of *voluntas*, the moral self—that finds us morally capable and implicated in reality. "Where are you?"

* * * *

If pride is self-assertion in defiance of God, then its consequence is distortion of objective reality on the one hand, and evasion of the subjective authority of conscience on the other ("subjective" in the sense of being inwardly communicated). Put another way, pride displaces the self before God, effectively shutting down communication with God. As Augustine remarks, "What else is pride, after all, but leaving the inner sanctum of conscience [*deserto secretario conscientia*] and wishing to be seen outwardly as what in fact one is not?" (*GRM* II.5.6).

Having "turned their backs on [God] … to love what is their very own" Adam and Eve became ashamed and quickly "hid themselves at themselves" (*GRM* II.16.24). In so doing they suppressed a capacity for awareness that locates the self in the way things are. The resulting split in their inner sanctum occasions their dismissal; they cannot abide in the presence of truth. Pride displaces conscience as the place of the self. The result is that humanity, now estranged from itself, begins to lose its bearing regarding the true and the false. It follows that in order to repair that estrangement, humanity must recover and re-enter the place of conscience.

In this reading, Augustine draws upon a prior tradition that interpreted Adam's fall as evasion of God (cf. Tertullian, *Adversus*

Marcionem II.25; Ambrose, *De Paradiso* 14.70). What he then appears to add is a clear articulation of the role played by pride in displacing moral conscience (for his legacy on conscience, see Fortin 1970; Svensson 2013). Affirming human beings have a desire to find truth, he observes that when truth confronts the errors of humanity, humans desire nothing more than to deny and resist it. It appears as if truth is not desired after all, or rather that it is mixed up in a "bundle of loves" (Gregory 2008: 21, 256). The most penetrating insight into this theme appears later, in *Confessions* book X, when Augustine delves more deeply into the human moral condition. After declaring that with humans there is still a little light, he embarks on an unveiling of the divided human heart.

> Why, though, does "truth engender hatred," why does a servant of yours who preaches the truth make himself an enemy to his hearers [Jn. 8:40; Gal. 4:16], if the life of happiness, which consists in rejoicing over the truth, is what they love? It must be because people love truth in such a way that those who love something else wish to regard what they love as truth and, since they would not want to be deceived, are unwilling to be convinced that they are wrong. They are thus led into hatred of truth for the sake of that very thing which they love under the guise of truth. They love truth when it enlightens them, but hate it when it accuses them [Jn. 3:20; 5:35]. In this attitude of reluctance to be deceived and intent to deceive others, they love truth when it reveals itself but hate it when it reveals them. Truth will therefore takes its revenge: when people refuse to be shown up by it, truth will show them up willy-nilly and yet elude them (*C* X.23.34).

For Augustine, truth hides as a punishment for sin; hence, God dismissed Adam and Eve from the Garden. "Notice the nice choice of words, *he sent him away*, not 'he shut them out,' so that [Adam] could be seen to be as good as shoved out by the pressure of his own sins [*ipso peccatorum suorum pondere*] to the only place he was fit for" (*GRM* II.22.34). The remarkable reality captured here is that humanity can be torn, split up by desires, and rendered incapable. For despite good intentions they fail to order love, confining a love of truth to their limited perceptions. The love of truth is still there in the loves they now express—for Augustine firmly believes in the continuity of all loves (Babcock 1991: 59; Gregory 2008: 257)—

but its expression yields little in the way of good fruit; it is but a flicker in the darkness of the night.

Yet, that flicker also holds the self in place, for "a little while yet there is light for human beings; let them walk in it, yes, let them walk, lest the darkness closes over them" (C X.23.33). It is a path that passes through and embraces moral conscience, the place where God will meet us and restore us to ourselves.

Locating Augustine in *Confessions* VIII

To reinforce our reading of Genesis 3, along with the emphasis we give to the conscience, we turn now to Augustine's famous account of his conversion; his account of how he struggled to, as he puts it, "surrender .... myself to [God's] love" (*C* VIII.5.12). In *Confessions* book VIII, Augustine narrates this story by deploying key images from Genesis 3. Though not explicitly referenced, God's question at 3:9 can be heard whispering softly in our author's narration. The words of Abraham Heschel throw light on our path.

> It is a cry that goes out again and again. It is a small voice, not uttered in words, not conveyed in categories of the mind, but ineffable and mysterious, as ineffable and mysterious as the glory that fills the whole world. It is wrapped in silence; concealed and subdued, yet it is as if all things were the frozen echo of the question: *Where art thou?* (Heschel 2007 [1976]: 137)

So much is true in the case of Augustine, who at this moment arrives in the place of confession.

With its climax taking place in a Milanese garden—an image specifically chosen to recall the Garden of Eden (Patterson 2016)—*Confessions* book VIII deploys many other images that suggest a deliberate modeling after the drama of Adam and Eve. In this case we read it as a return to Adam's place. God has opened the question once again to Augustine, "Where are you?," revealing where he stands versus where he ought to stand. Where Adam failed to step up and claim his true place, here Augustine begins to step forth and claim it for himself. A crucial moment takes place when he begins to confront himself. As he listens to Ponticianus tell of

St. Anthony, he finds he cannot move from the place where he is. He is stuck, thank God, and the truth begins to claim him:

> Ponticianus went on with his story; but, Lord, even while he spoke you were wrenching me back toward myself, and pulling me round from that standpoint behind my back [Jer. 2:27] which I had taken to avoid looking at myself. You set me down before my face [Ps. 49:21], forcing me to mark how despicable I was, how misshapen and begrimed, filthy and festering. I saw and shuddered. If I tried to turn my gaze away, he went on relentlessly telling his tale, and you set me before myself once more, thrusting me into my sight that I might perceive my sin and hate it [Ps. 35:3]. I had been aware of it all along, but I had been glossing over it, suppressing it and forgetting it. (C VIII.7.16)

For so long having refused to admit his condition, he begins to re-establish responsible contact with the truth. Set down "before my face" and made aware of his iniquity, "naked," he identifies self-deception as the root of his sickness. "I had been aware of it ... " he writes, now able to admit it. Why had he failed to admit it before? Why is he able to admit to it now? Possibly, his ability to confess at this moment is the result of his unwillingness and inability to move. He is stuck; he cannot and wills not to hide. Standing here in the place of moral conscience (see below), he collapses the distance between himself and himself. From the depths of self-deception he emerges through conscience, which discloses the secrets that were buried from his view: "one self hiding a guilty secret, and the other self sharing it" (Sorabji 2014: 36). He is no longer hiding himself from himself. His confession is the act of both mending and exposing, laying bare the sinful divisions that tear up his heart. Though yet to arrive, he has certainly arrived somewhere; and this is the place held in place by God's question, "Where are you?"

As the story plays out, so does the storyline of Genesis 3. Emotionally beside himself Augustine recalls his position. Overcome by fearful shame he was "stripped naked in my own eyes and my conscience challenged me within: 'Where is your ready tongue now?'" (C VIII.7.18). The echoes of Genesis 3 are unmistakably clear. As God called Adam to reveal his place so God calls Augustine to the place Adam abandoned. The difference is Augustine has nowhere to hide and nothing to say anymore in his defense. His journey at this point takes a turn for the better: though not without enduring another painful separation. "In my secret heart you stood by me, Lord, redoubling my lashes of fear and shame in the severity of your mercy, lest I give up the struggle and that slender, fragile bond that remained not be broken after all, but thicken again and constrict me more tightly" (C VIII.11.25).

Loosening and casting off the chains of deception finally allows him to step forth and claim his location. He declares "Here I am" (O'Donovan 2014: 33) in response to God's call, abandoning his fig-leaves for the tears of confession. Consequently, beneath a fig tree planted in a garden he begins to let Scripture take control of his story. He writes,

> I flung myself down somehow under a fig tree and gave free rein to the tears that burst from my eyes like rivers, as an acceptable sacrifice to you [Ps. 50:19]. Many things I had to say to you, and the gist of them, though not the precise words, was: "O Lord, how long? [Ps. 6:4]. How long. Will you be angry for ever? Do not remember our age-old sins [Ps. 78:5,8]." For by these I was conscious of being held prisoner. (C VIII.12.28)

The "age-old sins" he refers to are his own, and also likely refer to the sins of Adam and Eve. His journey thus recapitulates the story of Adam while also amending the folly of Adam's response. By returning to conscience he corrects Adam's posture and is now standing upright (*erectus*) in possession of reason (*compos rationis*). Better yet, he is reduced to his knees and to tears which is precisely the most reasonable upright posture he can adopt. It now takes one word from the Epistle to the Romans (vv. 13–14; see below) to set him on course for a life in God's home. "I had no wish to read further, nor was there need. No sooner had I reached the end of the verse than the light of certainty flooded my heart and all dark shades of doubt fled away" (C VIII.12.29).

Nor is his conversion merely a one-off event, but a cycle he repeats throughout his life as a Christian. In fact, the cycle plays out in his writings from the very first dialogue that acknowledges the authority of Christ (*The Academics*), to the very first treatise that defends the true religion (*True Religion*), to the very first study of the problem of evil in which Augustine attempts to re-enter Adam's place through the will (*Free Choice of the Will*).

Locating Christ in the early works

Romans 13:14 admonished Augustine to "*put on the Lord Jesus Christ, and make no provision for the flesh or the gratification of your desires.*" The impact of this verse has attracted considerable attention from scholars studying Augustine's early biography and theology. Biographically, some question when Augustine actually read it, as the verse is never referenced until later in his career. After a century of debating its historical veracity most scholars hold together at least two distinct claims: first, that Augustine had a conversion experience, one that included (likely) Romans 13; and second, that the account that he gives of that experience (in *Confessions* and elsewhere) does not adhere to modern standards of historical autobiography. Instead, Augustine uses his narrative of conversion as a lens through which to magnify important aspects of the experience. It may follow that his narrative does not accurately reflect events; but more likely shows him beginning to draw insights from events that he genuinely experienced but did not fully understand.

In any case, for this study our approach to this topic is to engage the theological question of the location of Christ. Rather than asking what Christ is to Augustine, that is, as a matter of Christological formulation, we explore how and where Christ shows up in Augustine as the latter ventures forth to "put on the Lord Jesus Christ." In so doing, we follow a prominent trend in recent studies that has represented Augustine as "the consummate teacher" (C. Harrison 2006: 223; cf. Kolbet 2009; Topping 2012): a writer more committed to the journey of faith than to propounding doctrines of the faith he embraces.

As for how Augustine put on the Lord Jesus Christ, we observe two aspects in the following Chapters: first, his attempt to imitate Christ in his method (Christ as Method), and second, his identification of Christ as the true teacher (Christ as Form).

Christ as Method. In *Confessions* book VII, after his encounter with the "books of the Platonists," Augustine explores the major differences between Platonism and Christianity. Among the verses he cites concerning the sacrifice and forgiveness of Christ—themes largely absent from his early works, as we note below—he lands on a passage in Matthew 11 that captures Christ's humility and benevolence to humanity. He writes:

For you [God] have *hidden these matters from the sagacious and shrewd, and revealed them to little ones* [Mt. 11:25], so that those who toil under heavy burdens may come to him and he may give them relief, because he is gentle and humble of heart [Mt. 11:28]. He will guide the gentle aright and teach the unassuming ways, for he sees our lowly estate and our labor, and forgives all our sins. As for those who are raised on stilts of their loftier doctrine, too high to hear him calling, *Learn of me, for I am gentle and humble of heart, and you shall find rest for your souls* [Mt. 11:29], even if they know God, they do not honor him as God or give him thanks; their thinking has been frittered away into futility and their foolish hearts are benighted, for in claiming to be wise they have become stupid (*C* VII.9.15).

Setting aside the reference to the forgiveness of Christ, here he draws attention to the humility of Christ, and specifically to his mission to stoop down and raise us up. By observing our toil and meeting us where we are, Christ lifts the "heavy burden" of our sinful futile ways. Matthew 11 resurfaces in book VII to highlight the Platonists' failure to obey Christ. "No one there hearkens to a voice calling, *Come to me, all you who struggle*. They [Platonists] are too scornful to learn from him, because he is gentle and humble of heart ..." (*C* VII.21.27). Evidently, one of the aspects unique to Christianity is its method of engaging and re-forming human souls. It is a method that lifts the burden of the fallen human lover not by preaching from on high the abstruse truths of religion, but by *meeting* the fallen lover on the road to wisdom and happiness.

Christ as Form. As Augustine famously reveals at the end of *The Teacher* (AD 388–9), no human being is the teacher of other humans. Rather, everyone learns from the Teacher within whom he later identifies the Word of God himself, Christ (*mag.* 13.46). As the "Form" by which our being is formed and re-formed, Christ gives us to ourselves in our knowing and our willing. His restorative function as Teacher and Form serves to underwrite Augustine's ethics and Christian philosophy. We are what we are because of Christ who gave us form, and we become what we must because of Christ who reforms us. Moreover, in naming Christ as the one "true philosophy" [*philosophia vera*] (Holte 1962; Djuth 2007), as the "voice" and "visage" of philosophy [*philosophiae vox et facies*] (*TA* II.3.8–9; O'Connell 1994), and as the "Virtue of God and Wisdom of God" [*virtus et sapientia Dei*] (1 Cor. 1:24; *TA* II.1.1),

Augustine underscores how Christ comprehensively embodies true knowledge through his enfolding and completing ancient philosophical wisdom. As Michael Cameron puts it, "Christ for Augustine was less a theological proposition and more *a way of seeing*. He was not preoccupied with exactly defining the constitution of Christ's person in two natures ... [rather] *Christ for us* wove himself into the warp and woof of Augustine's thought" (Cameron 2012: 12). Compare the modern theologian: "the Christological question begins not with *who* is the Christ or *what* is the Christ; it begins with *where* is the Christ ... it begins with an analysis of the operations whereby Christ is made known to us. And in being made known we participate in Him" (Ward 2005: 1; emphasis original).

Consequently, when Augustine calls readers to philosophy and specifically when he begs them to wake and arise (*evigilare*, *excitare*, *surgere*, etc.; Chapter 3), he is assuming that philosophy finds its full realization in the act of confessing Christ the Virtue and Wisdom of God. For the lover of wisdom who begins to awaken has begun to hear the voice and see the face of Truth itself. He has begun to regain his position in Adam and to put on Christ as the Form of all things. "He came forth, you see, as the form or shape of all things, supremely achieving the One, from whom he is, so that all other things that are, insofar as they are like the One, become so through that form or shape" (*TR* 43.81).

* * *

Although no one would deny Christ's significance to Augustine, some scholars question precisely *how* Christ was significant. In terms of the early works they propose the following thesis: not only did Augustine have an immature Christology, but he failed to distinguish properly between Platonic "presumption" and Christian "confession" (*C* VII.20.26). He failed, that is, to become a true Christian in accordance with the standards he would hold in the future. The latest iteration of this centuries-old thesis is an impressive recent study of Augustine's early works. Though its author Brian Dobell is not sold on his thesis—at least, he has his doubts about so provocative a claim—he does the service of defending it with care and precision to propose that Augustine *did not espouse an orthodox Christology in AD 386, and did not arrive at one until the year AD 395* (Dobell 2009: 23ff). In other words, the period to which this study is devoted, the period that begins (ostensibly) with our author's conversion to faith (as reported in C VIII, as traditionally interpreted), is possibly not the period of an emerging Christian philosophy (much less a Christian moral self), but instead a fatally flawed first attempt at such a philosophy.

Moreover, Dobell contends that Augustine, fully aware of this, confessed to its truth in the pages of *Confessions*. Looking back on this period as a newly appointed Bishop, he set out to re-invent himself by writing *Confessions* and slipping a few hints as to his former incorrect view: namely, by admitting in *Confessions* book VII that "it was later still [*aliquanto posterius*] that I learned how sharply divergent is Catholic truth from the falsity of Photinus with respect to the teaching that the Word was made flesh" (C VII.19.25). How long it to took him to recognize his error is a question that has animated a select group of scholars. Over against its traditional dating of a few brief months, Dobell argues that the phrase left ambiguous by Augustine, "it was later still" (or "it was only some time later"), in fact stretches nearly a decade across Augustine's early career; from AD 386 to AD 395, Dobell argues he "would have been following the Platonic path of presumption rather than the Christian path of confession" (Dobell 2009: 23).

An extraordinary claim demands extraordinary evidence; and Dobell marshals impressive evidence in his book. His argument does not hinge on a stand-alone statement but builds on a total re-framing of the book VII narrative, in addition to close readings of Augustine's early works. Suffice it to say the old ghost of Lord Alfaric—the infamous scholar who first claimed Augustine's conversion in AD 386 was to Neoplatonism, not to Christianity—still lurks. In taking note of Dobell, though, I want to express clearly that our aim is not to decipher the exact nature of Augustine's beliefs. Instead, we want to attend to how and where Christ is manifest, allowing that to signal where Augustine wants us to be. A deeper study of the sources and assumptions of this period would take us far afield from our purpose in this book. At the same time, having noted this ambiguity around Christ, I suggest that the journey to becoming a moral self also involves coming to terms with the location of Christ. In that spirit, let us conclude by turning very briefly to an important opening moment in Augustine's early works. It is a story of an ill-fated climb up a mountain that reveals new insight on the place of the self: or rather, new insight on the self's displacement.

Whatever deficiencies may attach to his early Christology, Augustine did not fail to recognize the dangers of pride (*superbia*). In the opening frame of his early dialogue *The Happy Life* (AD 386), he tells of three voyagers on a journey to the happy life, whom he identifies as people "whom philosophy can embrace." The details of these voyagers will occupy us later, but what is notable is how our author, after profiling their voyages, presents each as facing a common obstacle: a mountain. He describes this mountain as "wrapped in deceitful light," offering unwitting voyagers "a place to dwell." Those who ascend it are taken in by its "promises to satisfy their longing for the happy life," and in turn end up delighting in the vantage point it offers, "from which they can look down on the rest." In contrast, Augustine identifies another set of voyagers who seek out shelter in "the place of security" [*locum securitatis ostendunt*]. These men instead choose to draw close to philosophy, resisting the attractive heights of the towering mountain. This mountain is then identified as the sin of intellectual pride:

> For what other mountain does reason want to be understood as something to be feared by those who are approaching or by those who have already entered philosophy except the proud pursuit of empty glory [*superbum studium inanissimae gloriae*] that has nothing full and solid within, so that it pushes under and swallows up those walking on it who are puffed up with pride [*inflatos*] and once it has wrapped them in darkness it snatches away from them the shining home which they had scarcely glimpsed. (*THL* 1.3)

The two groups distinguished in this metaphor are important. The first group is obviously the one full of pride, and likely refers to the Academics if not the Platonists (Testard 1958: 167, 168; see Chapter 3, section "Seeking and doubting"). The second group is the one that is devoted to philosophy, and probably refers to Augustine along with those at Cassiciacum (see Chapter 3). Augustine is also clear on the consequences for each. Those who ascend end up giving up their journey, prematurely satisfying their desire for the happy life. Whereas those who choose to enter the place of security (i.e. the Church, if not Christ) end up finding their way into the region of the happy life (the "harbor of philosophy"). The mountain thus stands as a major impediment to fulfilling the central command at the heart of philosophy, "ask, seek, knock" (Mt. 7:7). As we shall see, Augustine's goal is to call many lovers to descend and "come down" from their lofty heights above; such is the way of the one true philosophy. "Come down, that you may ascend, ascend even to God, for you have fallen in your attempts to ascend in defiance of God."

3

Engaging the Despair of Skepticism

"The Academics"

In this chapter, the first of three pathways through Augustine, we embark on Augustine's early engagement with the Skeptics: alternatively called the Academics or Academicians of the New Academy. Our aim is to examine how these skeptical philosophers serve to advance Augustine's journey to reclaim the moral self. By focusing on Augustine's early dialogue *The Academics* (AD 386; often referred to as *Against the Academics*), we propose that Augustine seeks to engage the Academics by *imitating* their methods in pursuit of the truth.

In an early letter commenting on *The Academics* (AD 387), Augustine clarifies his aim was *not* to attack the Academics. "After all, how would the authority of such great men fail to disturb me, if I did not believe that they stood for a far different view than is commonly believed?" (*L* 1.1). Believing that the Skeptics secretly espoused the teachings of Plato (especially his immaterialism), he suggests that they trotted out their skepticism as a decoy, or a smokescreen, both to confuse and disorient certain materialist philosophies (e.g., Stoicism and Epicureanism). It is now, however, time to reveal their secret, for their tactic has caused a great deal of distress. As Augustine explains, "But now there is so great a shrinking from toil and so great a lack of interest in the fine arts that, as soon as people hear that the most intelligent philosophers thought that nothing can be grasped as true, they cease to use their mind and leave it in the dark for eternity" (L 1.2).

The smokescreen has come at a cost, he says, having led some people to give up on philosophy, and others to give in to "despair of finding the truth" [*desperatione veri*] (L 1.3; cf. TA II.3.8). If the Academics at one time protected philosophy they now pose a threat to its continuing success. But if so, why choose to imitate rather than attack? Augustine's motives become clear upon close examination of his narrowly defined goal for writing *The Academics*.

Stated briefly, in deciding to imitate the Skeptics Augustine enlists a powerful means for awakening true philosophers. Well aware that the Skeptics do not teach the "true philosophy" [*philosophia vera*] (cf. TA III.19.42), he is also fully aware of how useful they can be for provoking and inciting true desire for truth. His decision to imitate their methods of dialectic brings two distinct advantages to his present situation. First, it equips him with a time-honored strategy that will gain him the favor of his worldly patrons—many of whom are financing his retreat at Cassiciacum. Second, it offers flexibility and coverage for performing his true purpose of critiquing philosophy, conforming it inch-by-inch to the "authority of Christ" (TA III.20.43). To quote Catherine Conybeare on this two-pronged strategy: "The [Cassiciacum] dialogues are eminently suited to a liminal, enquiring state. Their genre bespeaks a pursuit that Augustine's patrons will find acceptably gentlemanly; at the same time, by foregrounding its artificiality, Augustine can use it to open up questions about the relationship of language to reality" (Conybeare 2006: 41).

To advance his objective of critiquing philosophy, Augustine enacts the Academic method of suspension of assent (Greek: *epochē*). In book I, he temporarily opts out of the dialogue by announcing his decision to play debate "referee" [*iudici*] (TA I.2.6). In book II, having refereed the debate so far, he intervenes to lament how the Academic teaching has made him less keen on the life of philosophy.

> [D]on't you know that up to now there is nothing I perceive to be certain? I'm prevented from searching for [truth] by the arguments of the Academicians. They somehow persuaded me of the plausibility ... that man cannot find the truth. Accordingly I had become lazy and utterly inactive, not daring to search for what the most ingenious and learned men weren't permitted to find (TA II.9.23).

To read this statement as a personal confession is to miss what is interesting about the response. By adopting the *persona* of an aspiring skeptic ("imitating" them) Augustine is modeling the *implications* of embracing skeptical philosophy (cf. Douglass 1996; Conybeare 2006). These implications include laziness and indifference toward the truth, placing the skeptic perilously close to despair of finding truth. In so doing Augustine is trying to confront the Skeptics by exploring how *they* confront *us* as lovers. To the extent that we yield to such "ingenious and learned men," to that extent do we falter in the life of philosophy.

Rather than dismiss the Academics *tout court*, Augustine thinks it may be necessary and even beneficial to engage them directly at the risk of despair. Consider this his drawing close to the void of despair, and from there reconceiving the assumptions of philosophy. Engaging the Skeptics for the goal of illumination (Curley 1997; Harding 2006), he will attempt to deliver readers to a form of creaturely "knowing" that will lay the basic foundation for a Christian philosophy. It all begins with awakening desire within, understood by Augustine as a response to the command of Christ: "ask, seek, knock" (Mt. 7:7; cf. *TA* II.3.9).

Seeking and doubting

Behind Augustine's argument both *for* and *against* the Skeptics lies a verse that is foundational for his early Christian philosophy; and one we have already become familiar with in this book: "Ask and you shall receive; seek and you shall find; knock and the door will be opened to you" (Mt. 7:7). This section examines the *command* in this verse, "ask, seek, knock," as used to justify our author's imitational approach to the Skeptics—at least to a point. First, we turn to two opening addresses that are dedicated to Augustine's patron Romanianus. As Augustine introduces the location of Romanianus, he reveals how the Skeptics have proved most effective in invigorating Romanianus for the one true happy life.

* * * *

Where is Romanianus? Not at Cassiciacum, not with Augustine, and not within the fold of faithful Catholics *thanks* to Augustine.

Alas, having listened to Augustine years ago, he is now a faithful "hearer" in the Manichean sect. He must be puzzled therefore by Augustine's recent decisions: to retire from his post as a teacher, first of all, abandoning a career long supported by Romanianus; and then to abandon the religion he once promoted to Romanianus, and even return to his once derided childhood faith (*TA* II.2.5). That Augustine feels responsible on both these accounts is clear by his deference to his long-suffering friend. And yet, owing to circumstances beyond their control he perceives an opportunity to amend past mistakes. If Romanianus, he thinks, will only listen once again, he will come perhaps to hunger for the same Christian truth; that is his hope.

To proceed, another piece to this backstory is required. Looking back at this period in *Confessions* book IX, Augustine recalls the bitter feelings he had felt toward the Manichees. Turning to the Psalter and specifically Psalm 4, he would vent his frustration through these powerful words of Scripture. He read in Psalm 4:3–4, "*How long will you be heavy-hearted? Why love emptiness and chase falsehood? Be sure of this: the Lord has glorified his Holy One.*" And he responded: "yet for so long I had been anything but sure, and had loved vanity and chased falsehood, and so I trembled as I heard these words, for they are addressed to the kind of person I remembered myself to have been" (*C* IX.4.9). The person he had been was of course a Manichee, and Psalm 4 helps to pinpoint the error of his ways. Now, under the easy yoke and light burden of Christ (Mt. 11) he is free from the vanity and heavy-heartedness of false love. His one wish however as he prays through these verses is that the Manichees might also come to "weary of their starvation," joining the lament of "the many" in Psalm 4:6, "Who will show us good things" [*Quis ostendet nobis bona?*]. Here, he says he prayed for his former co-religionists to experience the same longing that had brought him to faith. If only they would ask God to show them good things they might receive the hopeful message in Psalm 4:7, "Let us answer [the many], and let them hear the truth: *The light of your countenance has set its seal upon us, Lord* [Ps. 4:7]. We are not that Light which illumines every human being [Jn. 1:9], but by you we are illumined, so that we who were once darkness may become light in you [Eph. 5:8]" (*C* IX.4.10). In fact, that Augustine had the Manichees in view, and that he offered Psalm 4:6 specifically on their behalf, lead us to suggest that in this period he not only thought about the Manichees, but also tried to reach them through his philosophical dialogues.

To support this claim we consider his portrayal of the location of Romanianus in relation to philosophy. In his first dedicatory address (book I) he reveals a new development: Romanianus is beginning to show desire for the happy life. Having suffered recent setbacks in worldly affairs he is contemplating new directions in pursuit of true wisdom. His friend can hardly believe it and declares:

> Well, then I ask you who [*quisquam*], Romanianus! Who [*quisquam*] would dare to mention another happy life to you, one that alone is the happy life. Who [*quisquam*] could persuade you that not only were you not happy, but that you were especially unhappy in seeming to yourself not happy at all? How rapidly you have come to realize this now, with the many great misfortunes you have endured. (*TA* I.1.2)

Of course, he can believe it as a matter of divine providence, which is likely the "who" to whom he slyly refers. If his rhetoric is inflated it is inflated for a purpose, for he is trying to push his friend over the edge to philosophy. He is trying to "wake up" Romanianus from sleep, securing his commitment to his newfound desire:

> Therefore, that divine element in you [*divinus in te*], whatever it may be ... that element, I say, which has been lulled to sleep by the lethargy of this life, a hidden providence [*providentia secreta*] has decided to awaken [*excitare*] by the various hard reverses you have suffered. Wake up! Wake up I beg you! [*evigila, evigila, oro te*]. (*TA* I.1.3)

His resounding charge to awaken sets the agenda for the dialogue, which is centered on a still-infant desire for the happy life. What to make of his appeal to a "divine element within," literally a *divinity within* Romanianus? It is arguable this phrase is an innocent embellishment meant solely to dramatize the power of reason. It is true that such phrases often appear in ancient literature, even finding their way into the writings of Ambrose (Gerber 2012: 82, 83; 92–100). Although they do not automatically carry ontological weight (conflating human and divine), some scholars argue this is precisely the case here: admonishing Romanianus to wake up from within, Augustine, following Plotinus (or Cicero; Cary 2000: 111–114), presupposes the soul's divinity. If so, then Augustine has departed from orthodoxy, if not actually failed to grasp the orthodox view. And of course, this could threaten to undermine his project not only theologically but morally as well.

Tabling this debate for the moment (we return to it in Chapter 4, section "Turning outside in"), let us focus on two other terms in the passage, *providentia* and *evigilare*. Evidently, Augustine holds that in the case of Romanianus current events are not random but the result of a personal agency: a *who* not a *what*. Moreover, that agency has but one goal in view, to awaken Romanianus from the "lethargy of this life." Combining *providentia* with the verb *evigilare* draws attention to another traveling story Augustine tells, this from his companion work *The Happy Life*. In this work he profiles three different groups of voyagers presented as each capable of living the philosophical life (Chapter 2, section "Turning outside in"). The first and third groups form a notable contrast in that the former quickly reaches the shore of the happy life (e.g., Platonists), while the latter seems to dally in pursuit of celestial bodies (e.g., Manichees) (*THL* 1.2). Between these is a second group modeled on Romanianus. Though this group initially sets out in search of the happy life, it steers its course gradually to "vain pleasures and honors." Similarly, Augustine pokes at his friend Romanianus for having to suffer the constant temptations of vanity and pretense: "Riches were showered upon you from every side. They began to engulf your youthful spirit, leading you to the eager pursuit of whatever appeared beautiful and worthwhile in their seductive whirlpools. When you were practically drowning, you were snatched away by those winds of fortune that are considered favorable" (*TA* I.1.1). The same favorable winds reappear in *The Happy Life*, in the form of "a violent storm and hostile wind." By this wind the second voyagers abandon their "empty concerns" and convert all their focus to the "books of wise and learned men." And then, something remarkable happens to them, for in reading these books they "wake up [*evigilant*] … in the harbor of philosophy" (*THL* 1.2). Signaling this event is not the end but the beginning Augustine reveals the next step in the journey of Romanianus: reading books. Which books he is referring to is the question, however. Given the important role books played in his conversion (Stock 2010: 39; citing Nock 1993: 179), we can assume he had some specific ones in mind.

As it happens he mentions several books in the period. The first and obvious candidate, "the books of the Platonists," are cited in *The Happy Life* as "a few precious books of Plotinus" (*THL* 1.4; cf. *TA* II.2.5). Despite their effect on Augustine's intellectual journey, they arrive rather late in the dialogue *The Academics*. The second plausible candidate is Cicero's *Hortensius*. Not only does Augustine assign this book at Cassiciacum (*TA* I.1.5), but he also praises the book for setting him aflame with "love of philosophy" (*THL*. 1.4). That said, a third candidate also suggests itself: *The Academics*. Though Augustine might not call its author wise or learned, the dialogue is uniquely tailored to Romanianus' condition. It is even given a remit that is identical to *Hortensius*: "a foretaste to incite you to cling to [the breasts of philosophy] and suckle the more eagerly" (*TA* I.1.5). Moreover, knowing his plan is to imitate the Skeptics—and recall he earlier praised them (playfully) as "the most ingenious and learned men"—it is plausible that Augustine wants to blaze a new trail by crafting his own protreptic to *replace* the *Hortensius* (Foley 1999: 63). After all, if his goal is conversion to Christ, what use is a text that fails to mention the name of Christ?

If *The Academics* is the book for Romanianus, then, why specifically the Academics as its main interlocutor? Another clue comes to the fore in the second dedicatory address (book II), in which Augustine presents two major obstacles to philosophy. The first major obstacle is the Academics themselves. They claim that it is not possible for anyone to find truth, thus threatening the legitimacy of the *promise* of philosophy. The second major obstacle, and the more immediate threat, is the Manichean claim to have already "found some truth" (*TA* II.3.8). This threatens not the legitimacy but the necessity of philosophy, and more specifically the philosophical command to "ask, seek, knock." In treating the Manichees as the more immediate threat, Augustine anticipates the critique he will level in later texts: the Manichees do not find because they fail to seek, being more bent on "captious fault-finding" than a "spirit of reverent inquiry" (Chapter 2, section "Locating Adam in Genesis 3"). Whereas despite their flirting with "despair at finding [wisdom]" [*desperatio inveniendi*], the Academics have *emboldened* Romanianus on his quest: "You have often been angry at the Academicians, the more severely, the less knowledgeable you were about them; the more gladly, *because you were led on* by your love of the truth" (*TA* II.3.8; emphasis added).

It thus appears that the criterion for distinguishing the two is which group more incites a desire to find the truth (or wisdom). The Academic Skeptics, with their secret and suggestive beliefs, beat out the Manichees with their inflated superiority. For Augustine, it all comes down to their effect on Romanianus.

> As for the second obstacle, namely that you perhaps assume that you have found some truth, despite the fact that you were searching and doubting [*quaerens et dubitansque*] when you left us—if any superstition has returned to your mind, it will surely be cast out once I've sent you a discussion among ourselves concerning religion [*disputationem de religione*] or when I talk many things over with you in person. (*TA* II.3.8; he is alluding to *True Religion*)

Locating his friend in a place of "searching and doubting," Augustine offers a clue to his motive in this period. The Skeptics have unsettled Romanianus the Manichee ("doubting) and predisposed his obedience to the command to philosophize ("searching"). Looking back at the experience of Augustine with the Skeptics further illumines his decision to engage their philosophy.

※ ※ ※ ※

In *Confessions* book VI, Augustine recalls his struggle to endure the philosophical challenge of the Academic Skeptics. Deploying similar imagery that we find in *The Happy Life*, he portrays his soul foundering in a sea of different opinions:

> Yet I was walking a dark and slippery path, searching for you outside myself I had sunk to the depth of the sea [Ps. 67:23], I lost all faith and despaired of ever finding the truth [*desperabam de inventioni veri*] .... [My mother] found me ... beset by mortal danger as I despaired of discovering the truth [*desperatione indagandae veritatis*] .... I had meanwhile been brought to my present point of wavering; and [my mother] foresaw with certainty that I would have to pass through a still more dangerous condition—a crisis, as the physicians call it—on my way from sickness to health. (*C* VI.1.1)

Being tossed by severe winds of intellectual doubt Augustine landed dangerously close to the void of despair. It was then that he encountered Ambrose's preaching and teaching, which began to treat the sickness that was afflicting his heart. What he says about this sickness bears directly on Romanianus. It was rooted in a perverse form of arrogant pride, the kind of pride that preferred disputation over dialogue. As he explains at different points the disposition he embodied: "Not yet had I begun to pour forth my groans to you in prayer, begging you to help me; rather was my mind intent on searching and restlessly eager for argument." "Since I did not know how your [divine] image could exist in us I would, given the chance, have knocked at the door [Mt. 7:7] and proposed my question about how this doctrine was to be believed, instead of opposing it with insults ..." (*C* VI.3.3). "I had been deluded and beguiled by assurances that falsehoods were certain, and [I] had in my headstrong, childish error babbled about such very dubious things as though they were proven. Later it became clear to me that these tenets were false ..." (*C* VI.4.5). What loosened the chains of such vanity and pride? At least in the beginning, it was the Academic Skeptics, who had placed him precariously at his "present point of wavering". If passing through the Skeptics had secured his recovery, it reasonably follows that perhaps in the wisdom of providence they could serve the same purpose for his friend Romanianus.

Seeking, not finding

Philosophy means love of wisdom. What does this involve? For Augustine, to love wisdom is to possess a restless heart, longing and striving for possession of what is sought. To seek wisdom is to adhere to the "logic" of desire implicit in the words of Christ in Matthew 7:7, "Seek and you shall find" (*TA* II.3.9). This logic can be divided into a command and a promise. First, we are invited to "ask, seek, knock," and second, we are assured that our striving is not in vain: "you *shall* find." The logic is implicit in the desire itself: we will not seek if we do not want to find, and nor will we seek if we believe we cannot find.

Unfolding this logic step-by-step in *The Academics*, Augustine cuts a sharp path through the Academic weeds. In book I, this path takes off from a simple question: do you *genuinely* desire wisdom, truth, happiness? The adverb underlines the area of dispute: yes, many claim to love wisdom and truth (happiness is taken for granted), but very few turn out to be *committed* to the pursuit. "Mention happiness," Augustine writes in the dialogue *On Order*,

> and all stand up, hands extended, to beg of you some alms as if they were poor wretches in the grip of a disease. But as wisdom begins to demand that they take themselves to the physician [Christ] and let themselves be cured by him, they return to their rags. Wasting away in the warmth of their rags, they scratch the itchy scabs of troublesome lust rather than submit to the physician's prescriptions ...

Switching metaphors he continues, "That excellent and most beautiful Spouse, however, seeks other men, or better, other souls not happy with just getting on [*non vivere ... satis sit*], but satisfied only with a happy life, and therefore worthy of his marriage bed" (*OO* I.8.24 [tr. Barruso]).

To become worthy of wisdom is the goal of philosophy, for philosophy can only prepare us for an encounter with wisdom. "Philosophy promises that this view to which I'm inviting you [Romanianus] ... will show itself to its genuine lovers [*veris amatoribus suis*]" (*TA* I.1.1). The condition for finding what we seek in philosophy is to occupy a place in which light can break through. It is to step forward and claim responsibility for our quest, responding to the "demand" placed on all of us by wisdom and truth. "Let us return to ourselves—let us, I say, devote our attention to philosophy, Romanianus" (*TA* II.3.8).

* * * *

In book I Augustine invites his two students, Trygetius and Licentius, to explore the philosophical relation between happiness and truth. His opening questions serve to clarify their positions; he begins by asking, "Do you have any doubt that we ought to know the truth?" The two students deny any doubts in this area; in this they rightly obey the authority of Cicero. Augustine's next question presses them further: "Well ... if we can be happy while not apprehending the truth, do you the consider apprehension of the truth to be necessary?" Knowing truth is great but may be unnecessary, especially if our goal is to find the happy life. In response to this point Trygetius again channels Cicero: "*Surely we wish to be happy.*

If we can reach this condition without the truth, we don't need to search for the truth" (*TA* I.2.5). For Trygetius, the question is which desire is more basic: desire for happiness or desire for truth. If one can be fulfilled at the expense of the other we should consider if the other is essential after all. Although no one would deny his desire to be happy, very few learned philosophers can claim to know the truth. The question is, is it possible to gain happiness without truth? It is on this question that the two disagree.

In one corner stands Trygetius, who thinks happiness requires truth. In the other corner stands Licentius, who thinks the two can be separate. More exactly, Licentius agrees that we need to know the truth, but questions if *obtaining* it is necessary for happiness. In line with certain forms of Academic skepticism he holds that seeking truth, if conducted in a "perfect" manner, is not only necessary for the soul to be happy; it *is* happiness itself. "This *is* human happiness," he proclaims, "to search for the truth perfectly! This is to get a goal we can't go beyond. Therefore, anyone who searches for the truth less insistently than he should doesn't get to the goal of man." Indeed, he will try to defend the bolder claim that a failure to find truth does not lead to despair. "Anyone who takes pains to find the truth, to the extent that a man can and should, is happy—even if he were not to find it." Shocked by this view Trygetius stammers in retort: "Then man can't be happy ... How could he be, since he can't attain what he desires so greatly [*magnopere concupiscit*]?" (*TA* I.3.9). But in fact that is the question: how *greatly* he desires it. For perhaps his desire does not demand that much, and perhaps he can sate it by merely searching for the truth. It comes down to how he measures or ought to measure love's weight: not only what he "feels" about desire for truth, a "subjective" assessment, but also what the object might demand *from* him, an "objective" assessment. Needless to say, Augustine thinks that truth demands much, yet he will not intervene at this point to disclose it.

However, it is worth bringing forth his view here as preparation for exploring his approach to the Skeptics. Returning to this question in *The Happy Life*, Augustine mounts a brief argument *against* the Academics. Called by Christopher Kirwan "the argument from beatitude" (Kirwan 1989: 17–20), it holds that for a person to gain the happy life, it is necessary to bring his "strong desires" to fulfilment. No one can be happy with his desires unfulfilled; hence the Academics who greatly desire truth must in truth be unhappy in their failure to find it. Kirwan objects to this form of the argument. It is possible, he argues, to adjust one's desires to reflect the reality of their frustration or disappointment. If the skeptic cannot find what he says he is seeking, he could simply alter the conditions of his notion of happiness (Kirwan 1989: 20; cf. O'Daly 2001: 160). In this argument which centers on the skeptic's disposition, Kirwan sets the specific nature of the object aside. Desire for truth is not any old desire, but a desire for the end to all rationally intelligible ends (cf. Harding 2006: 249, 250, n7; Topping 2012: 118–120). Moreover, truth is unlike any other object; for Augustine, it demands something *from* a rational agent. It does not lie yonder as an inert thing-to-be-grasped; rather, it is written into the order of the universe ("the way things are"), the condition of the possibility of being, knowing, willing. In short, Kirwan misconstrues the force of this argument by ignoring which "object" endows love with its weight.

Moreover, to settle for less than the truth is to show that one's desire for the truth is not genuine. For Augustine, if we always implicitly desire the truth, we do not always assume responsibility for its search. The very fact that we desire truth at all, of course, is a testimony to the in-dwelling presence of the truth. "You stir us so that praising you may bring us joy, because you have made us and drawn us to yourself, and our heart is unquiet until it rests in you" (*C* I.1.1). It is perhaps this insight that lights up Trygetius as he responds to Augustine's little argument from beatitude: "I'm so glad that I have long been an opponent of the Academics. For, by some impulse of nature or, to speak more correctly, of God, I was still very much against them though I didn't know [*nesciens*] how they were to be refuted" (*THL* 2.14). Not knowing from what impulse he opposed the Academics, Trygetius knows enough to trace it back to God the Creator. In so doing he anticipates Augustine's answer to the Skeptics once the dialogue has accomplished what it sets out to do: make true philosophers through encounter with the truth.

* * * *

This reading not only clarifies Augustine's critique of the Skeptics. It also clarifies the purpose of book I in general. The purpose it turns out is not to declare winners and losers (though Trygetius gets the upper hand), but to commend both students for defending their beliefs. For example, Augustine singles out Trygetius' behavior to extoll how he "recovered and, with some noble firmness, leaped to the pinnacle of freedom [*verticem libertatis exsiliit*]" (*TA* I.9.24). Rather than just defer to the authority of Cicero, he seized on the opportunity to think his own thoughts, to take responsibility for his capacity for reason. "You were all so dedicated that I couldn't want more" (*TA* I.9.25). Once again, the entire occasion ties back to Augustine, specifically his experience reading Cicero as a budding philosopher.

Earlier, we mentioned the role of *Hortensius* as a forerunner and template for *The Academics*. In *The Happy Life*, Cicero's *Hortensius* is presented as the spark-plug igniting Augustine's quest for philosophy. It is the book that inflamed him with "such a love of philosophy that I planned to devote myself to her immediately." At the same time, Augustine describes how he was diverted from philosophy by a "childish superstition [that] frightened me away from the search itself." He is referring in this case not to the religion of Manichaeism, but to the anti-intellectualism of the North African Church (*TAB* 1.2; cf. O'Connell 1986: 15; citing Courcelle 1968). The Church's aversion to reason only left him discouraged and led to his desertion of Catholicism for Manichaeism. Before this, however, something else took place that forms the basic framework of his Cassiciacum period. Augustine declares that "after I had been made more upright [*factus erectior*], I scattered that fog and was convinced that I should yield to those who teach rather than who command obedience. I fell in with men to whom that light seen by the eyes was thought of as deserving worship among the higher divinities" (*THL* 1.4). The men in the last sentence are clearly the Manichees, yet what does he mean by "I had been made more upright"? The answer, we suggest, connects back to Cicero and the role he is to play now in *The Academics*.

Factus erectior refers to the impact of *Hortensius* (O'Connell 1986). It marks the moment when Augustine began to wake to philosophy by learning to stand upright and seize hold of reason. The verb *erigere* calls to mind the creation of Adam. As Augustine describes it, "The bodies of all animals ... do not have an upright posture [*erecta*] like the human body. And this signifies that our spirit also ought to be held upright [*erectum*], turned to the things above it, that is to eternal, spiritual realities" (*GRM* I.17.28). In the same passage this posture is tied to the divine image, which suggests the same doctrine may be afloat in *The Happy Life*. As for *factus*, R.J. O'Connell links it to the work of providence and order (O'Connell 1986: 28, 29). Divine providence ordained it that by reading *Hortensius*, Augustine would re-discover his position in Adam. He may also think that in engaging the Academics, of whom Cicero is a member, he is courting the same providence on behalf of Romanianus (see above).

Moreover, Augustine returns to this moment in *Confessions* to acknowledge more clearly God's role in the process. Various parts of the passage repeat prior claims: first, his emphasis on inflaming desire ("My God, how I burned, how I burned with longing ..."); second, his acknowledgement of his ignorance at the time ("I did not know [*nesciebam*] what you were doing with me"—compare with Trygetius' comment); third, his focus on philosophy as love of wisdom, and wisdom as God; fourth, his indictment of many a pagan philosopher, except of course Cicero (C III.4.8). As for Cicero, Augustine praises him for channeling Paul's wisdom (Col. 2:8–9) and for turning him away from many vain and pointless philosophies. Positively he singles out a line from *Hortensius* that apparently had impacted him greatly on his quest: "Nevertheless, the one thing that delighted me in Cicero's exhortation was the advice 'not to study one particular sect but to love and seek and pursue and hold fast and strongly embrace wisdom itself, wherever found.'" Notice Cicero's emphasis on the call to love and seek. Not only did Cicero channel the wisdom of Paul, he also apparently channeled the command of Christ to "ask, seek, knock" (as it happens, a favorite verse of the Manichees, whom Augustine soon encounters; cf. *TMWL* II.17.31). Augustine sharpens the irony of this inadvertent summons when claiming that despite Cicero's powerful call to philosophy, Cicero could not offer him a viable way forward. "One thing alone put a brake on my intense enthusiasm—that the name of Christ was not contained in the book." In truth, we are to understand that Christ was present, whereas Augustine was only beginning to be present to himself.

* * * *

Continuing with this connection between Cicero and Christ, especially Cicero's channeling of the command of Matthew 7:7, we propose that to understand *The Academics* we must recognize its focus on a specific form of skepticism: namely, Cicero's "mitigated skepticism" (cf. Catapano 2006; Thorsrud 2009: 84–101). Following Harald Thorsrud's account of Cicero's views, it appears that Cicero no only embraced the preceding Greek tradition, but also fundamentally altered it to fit his designs. The changes he wrought would change the way it was received and specifically altered the way it was interpreted by Augustine.

As Michael Foley has shown (Foley 1999), *The Academics* was written as a response to Cicero's *Academica*. As Augustine's sole source of knowledge of skepticism, *Academica* contains several innovations on the tradition. In relation to book I, the main innovation to highlight is Cicero's efforts to mitigate the Academic method: suspension of assent (*epochē*). According to Thorsrud, this mitigation followed the steps of Carneades. In response to Stoic objections to the Academic wise man, Carneades had invented the practical criterion of a "persuasive" impression (*to pithanon*). He reasoned that the wise man on certain occasions could give assent to such impressions if he desired. He believed this sufficed to meet the Stoic objection to the Academic wise man's life of inactivity (*apraxia*) (cf. Brittain 2006: xxiii; Thorsrud 2009: 75ff; *TA* II.10.32). Given how highly Cicero praised civic engagement (cf. *De officiis*) it is not at all surprising he would applaud Carneades' move. In advancing this criterion, Carneades changed Academic practice. Whereas *epochē* before had been identified *as* wisdom, such that the method was not only a method but the *goal*, Carneades conceived it as a temporary measure deployed in the service of the practical criterion. In short, *epochē* ceased to be an end-in-itself, and became the practical means to achieving another end.

Though Carneades' definition of this criterion is unclear—he left no writings (Obdrzalek 2006: 243–279, n. 2; Thorsrud 2009: 78–81)—it is clear that by the time Cicero arrived on the scene the criterion had begun to acquire epistemic status. No longer was skepticism absolute and uncompromising but instead had given way to a positive account of knowledge. To cement the transition, Cicero translated *to pithanon* with the epistemic terms *veri simile* and *probabilis*. In so doing, he arguably spelled the end of skepticism as a practice of negation and of pure dialectic. "Cicero ... translates Carneades' pithanon with the Latin probabile (i.e., probable or plausible) and sometimes veri simile (i.e., truth-like), and maintains that the sole purpose of the Academic argument pro and con is to 'draw out or formulate the truth or its closest possible approximation'" (Thorsrud 2009: 88; quoting Cicero, *Academica* 2.7). Correspondingly, Cicero lent credence to the view that one can make progress in the life of philosophy. Skepticism for him became a struggle to find the truth, even if the truth-like is the best one can do. In this way, he solidified the Academic method as a temporary posture toward competing claims to truth (Cicero, *Academica* II.29.93, II.34.108, II.36.114). It became a mere "tool" in the philosopher's toolkit enabling him to sift out the probable and the truth-like. Thorsrud explains,

> Rather than merely revealing larger portions of our ignorance, Cicero thinks the Academic method allows for progress towards the truth ... So Cicero uses the Academic dialectical method to accomplish both positive and negative ends: by revealing the strength of the opposed arguments it eliminates unwarranted confidence while establishing the degree to which one view is more probable than another. (Thorsrud 2009: 88, 93, 94)

Although the epistemic changes hold importance for Augustine—he seizes very quickly on the probable and the truth-like (see book II)—it is Cicero's mitigation of *epochē* that matters in terms of Augustine's interest in the "ethics of belief." Put simply, it reinforces his view of truth as that which demands lovers to seek *in order to* find. When Licentius tried to separate seeking and finding, he reached behind Cicero to an earlier skeptical tradition. Cicero for his part is clear about his objective: "I am burning with the desire to *discover* the truth and my arguments express what I really think. How could I not desire to *find* the truth when I rejoice if I find something truth-like?" (Cicero, *Academica* II.20.65; emphasis added).

By this admission, Cicero implies a further point. Philosophy has no space for any claim to "neutrality," for in seeking as in finding one is always in a place. One is always "on the way" to some end that one desires, even if that desire ends up settling for the truth-like (as it must for Cicero). For this reason Brian Harding can advance the bold claim that Cicero's philosophy has an inherent religious dimension:

> [For Cicero], at the time the initial choice for a philosophical life—and with it, adherence to a philosophical school—is made one is not in the position to know the truth, but only seeking the

truth. The philosopher, therefore, does not begin with the purity of reason but rather begins immersed in the heteronomous cave of received opinions, not yet fully understood. Philosophy, as the search for *rerum humanarum divinarumque scientiam* [Cicero's definition of wisdom] insofar as it begins with opinions, including partially understood philosophical doctrines, is always already *fides quaerens intellectum*. (Harding 2008: 9)

More precisely, his starting point is not *fides quarens intellectum*, but desire seeking truth through adherence to the truth-like (though it is not as provocative). For this reason, Cicero departs from the view of Licentius on the question of the philosopher's ability to avoid risk. Risk is inherent in the philosophical life (Thorsrud 2009: 95), and efforts to avoid it only inhibit one's search. Even so, Cicero leaves us still asking the question Augustine raises against the Skeptics in *The Happy Life*: Is it possible to settle with the truth-like not the truth? And if so, is it *true* to the desire for truth? Once again Cicero instructs us to "ask, seek, knock," but once again he can provide us no assurances in the search ("you shall find"). The absence of hope betrays the absence of faith which Augustine considers crucial to the true love of wisdom. We conclude with this point.

Seeking as praying

Cicero paves the way to the life of philosophy by calling all lovers to "ask, seek, knock." Cicero, however, cannot promise what is sought, and leaves the heart stammering and faltering under its weight. Who can show lovers to the truth that they desire?

This final section explores three moments in the period that mark decisive steps to reclaiming the moral self. The climax is a breakthrough in responsible self-knowing that delivers Augustine's readers to the prayer of Psalm 4:6, "Who will show us good things?" Only this time the prayer is slightly altered for context: "Who can show us the truth?," and the question directly related to the voice and visage of philosophy, Christ.

In book II, Augustine once again exhorts Romanianus: "Believe me—or rather, believe Him, for He says *Search and you shall find*— knowledge is not to be despaired of, and it will be clearer than those numbers are" (*TA* II.3.9). And admonishing him before this to pray for his journey, Augustine indicates *to whom* Romanianus' prayers should be directed: "I pray to the power and wisdom itself of God the Highest. What else is He whom the mysteries reveal to us as the Son of God?" (*TA* II.1.1). And before this, he reveals that Philosophy Herself—personified—has taken it upon Herself to reveal the true God. "Philosophy promises that [she] will display the true and hidden God, and now and again deigns to show us [*ostentare dignatur*] a glimpse of Him through the bright clouds [*per lucidas nubes*], as it were" (*TA* I.1.3; altering King's neutered translation). His reference to "clouds" is a metaphor for Christ (*GRM* II.4.5), and so is his appeal to the *descent* of Philosophy; that is, the Incarnation. Christ *is* the "voice" [*vox*] and the "visage" [*facies*] of Philosophy (*TA* II.3.7), prompting Augustine's surrender to this authority in book III: "Therefore, I'm resolved not to depart from the authority of Christ on any score whatsoever: I find no more powerful [authority]" (*TA* III.20.43). In light of this, we can agree with R.J. O'Connell that this period exhibits a "thoroughly religious and specifically Christian style of understanding which the recent convert labels with the term 'philosophy.'" We can also agree Augustine "clearly expected that both his companions at Cassiciacum as well as his eventual readers would be equally able to decode his message, if only they paid sufficient attention to the text" (O'Connell 1994: 68, 69). Having paid some attention to the text already, let us perform one more analysis of the last two books, plotting our way to the place of the moral self.

* * * *

The first decisive moment takes place in book II. Dominated for the most part by the New Academy's history, book II also features a critical moment for Licentius: the erstwhile defender of the Academic Skeptics will turn to embrace a Platonic account of human knowledge. The moment turns on a discussion of the probable and truth-like (Cicero's new terms). Augustine seizes on these terms to mount a challenge to the skeptic—this is him exploiting Cicero's mitigated skepticism. He puts to Licentius a basic problem drawn from Plato's *Meno*: the problem of apprehending the truth-like without the truth. It would seem one needs to know the truth to know the truth-like, for how can one recognize any likeness without it? He draws an analogy with a father–son relationship: "If a man unacquainted with your father were to see your brother and assert that he is like your father, won't he seem to you crazy or simple-minded?" (*TA* II.7.16). In this case, his analogy may serve a double function, appealing to Licentius *and* his father Romanianus. First, as Licentius is struggling to reply, Augustine reminds him of their purpose "to train you and to incite you to cultivate your mind" (*TA* II.7.17). Then, he cites his father as a primary example, encouraging *his* reflection on the problem from afar: "Yet surely no one will drink of philosophy more eagerly than your father, after so long a thirst. What if you saw him investigating and arguing these matters with us?" Yet rather than assuage the uncertainty of Licentius, this example only elevates his mounting frustration. Then, something happens that begins to turn the tables. Unable to contain his frustration anymore, Licentius breaks forth into an earnest honest prayer: "When, O God, shall I see this? Yet there is nothing we need despair [*desperandum*] of obtaining from You!" The outbreak marks a moment of decisive importance, one easily missed by the philosopher allergic to prayer. Everyone rallies around the hapless Licentius, and even Trygetius, his former opponent, offers up a light response: "Why shouldn't such an upstanding man want God to grant his prayer before he offers it? Have faith now, Licentius! You who cannot find anything to say in reply and still want to win seem to me to have little faith!" (*TA* II.7.18). He means it in jest, yet he also has a point. Lacking the faith to "win" what he seeks is the logical extension of Licentius' skepticism. His allegiance to skepticism had supported his search, but now seems incapable of sustaining it further. With the void of despair ever lurking in the shadows, Licentius is all but forced to offer prayer in response—not a bad thing. As the situation intensifies in *The Academics*, Augustine begins to step in and assume an active role.

He is preceded in this by his friend, Alypius, who has rejoined the group after a brief sojourn elsewhere. He states his intention to debate with Augustine as a service to the students in their search for the truth. Doing so, he says, will keep his pride in check (*TA* II.8.21), which reassures Augustine that the dialogue can proceed. He warns the present company that the stakes could not be higher. "[L]et childish tales be put beyond our reach! The matter at hand concerns our life, morality, and spirit" (*TA* II.9.22; cf. III.16.35). It is time to set aside playing the part of referee. It is time to get serious about the life of philosophy.

The Skeptics, he says, must be challenged in their skepticism, particularly their claim that it is impossible to know the truth. With Alypius agreeing to role-play the skeptic, Augustine sets out the terms for their ensuring debate:

> The only difference between my viewpoint and the viewpoint of the Academicians is that to them it seems plausible that the truth can't be found [*non posse*] whereas to me it seems plausible that the truth can be found [*posse*]. If they are only pretending, then ignorance of the truth is peculiar to me alone; otherwise, it is common to both. (*TA* II.9.23)

It is this contrast in possibilities, between *posse/non posse* and *probabilis/non probabilis*, that will frame Augustine's challenge to the Academic Skeptics. We return to it later.

At this point, Licentius undergoes a second breakthrough. He awakens to what Augustine wanted him to see, declaring, "Wait a moment, please. I'm catching a glimpse of something—a glimmer by which I see that so great an argument shouldn't be snatched away from [Augustine] so easily!" Eager to explain, he repeats the Platonic insight that perceiving the truth-like requires knowing the truth; therefore, the Academics are either foolishly mistaken, or concealing their views to accomplish some other end. Licentius concludes: "Well, nothing seems more absurd than for someone who doesn't know the truth to say that he's following something truth-like … But you, Carneades … since you say that you don't know any truth, on what grounds do you follow something truth-like?" (*TA* II.12.27). The mention of Carneades is significant, we suggest, and will come into play at the end of *The Academics*.

* * * *

Before venturing on the exchange between Alypius and Augustine we propose to take a detour to the end of *The Happy Life*. The hero in this dialogue is Augustine's mother Monica, whose (female) presence already mounts a challenge to philosophy (McWilliam 1990; Holte 1994; Conybeare 2006: 63–138). That said, she also appears to be more than a philosopher but an ideal representative of the Christian pilgrim's life. Standing for Mother Church, she embodies the Christian virtues of a life lived by faith and the piety of prayer. At the end of *The Happy Life* after a tedious to-and-fro, she will cut through the dross with a decisive spiritual clarity, leaving her so-called superiors dumbfounded in amazement.

The occasion is Augustine's Trinitarian account of the happy life; how the happy life, which consists in "full satiety of minds," acknowledges "that by which you are led into truth [Son], that truth which you enjoy [Father], and that through which you are joined to the highest limit [Spirit]." Monica springs forth in response to this point:

> My mother recognized these words, which were fixed deep in her memory, and, as though awakening [*evigilans*] into her faith, uttered joyously that verse of our priest [Ambrose]: "Cherish us as we pray, O Trinity," and added, "this is without doubt the happy life, and that life is perfect toward which we can, we must presume, be quickly brought through solid faith, lively hope, and burning love." (*THL* 4.35)

By deploying *evigilare* to describe Monica's breakthrough, Augustine identifies the end for which he strives in this period. That end is none other than faith, hope, and love, which grounds the young and old (the male and female, the intellectual and simple) in a common search for truth. He invokes this triad again in later texts, presenting faith, hope, and love as conditions for virtue (*OO* II.8.25) and wisdom (*TS* I.6.13). As we shall see, the virtue of hope takes on a significant role as Augustine develops his answer to the Academic Skeptics. However, it is also clear that he regards Monica's faith as a path far superior to the wrangling of the philosophers (*OO* II.17.45).

* * * *

Now comes the debate between Augustine and Alypius, a debate that also gives us Augustine's answer to the Skeptics. Augustine begins by restating the disagreement in book II:

> Therefore, the question between us is whether their arguments make it plausible [*probabile*] that nothing can [*posse*] be perceived and that one should not assent to anything. Now if you prevail [Alypius], I'll gladly yield. Yet if I can demonstrate that it's much more plausible [*probabilis*] that the wise man be able [*posse*] to attain the truth and that assent need not always be withheld, then you'll have no reason, I think, for refusing to come over to my view. (*TA* II.13.30)

Again the two terms *posse* and *probabilis* draw attention to the area he will look to exploit. He will seize on these terms and interrogate their basis, then propose their convertibility to the triad of faith, hope, and love. As he does, he will invite his interlocutor Alypius—and by extension Romanianus, Licentius, and us—to take responsibility for his search for the truth; to step off the platform of Academic *epochē* and dare the possibility that truth *can* be found. Or even dare that the truth has been found already, and by one who deigns to show it if we love it wholeheartedly (cf. Ps. 4:6). As we proceed, let us recall God's question in Genesis as indicative of the spirit behind the upcoming exchange: "Where are you, lover of wisdom who seeks to find the truth?"

In book III, the two men are serious about their quest. They agree that their task is "neither trivial nor superfluous, but necessary and of supreme importance: to search wholeheartedly for the truth" (*TA* III.1.1). This agreement stood at the heart of books I and II, and continues to prop up the debate in book III. With it, however, Augustine raises some new questions. First, he distinguishes between the "wise man" [*sapiens*] and "philosopher" [*philosophus*], and asks Alypius to explain the difference between them. What is it that makes one wise, the other not? To Alypius, the difference amounts to something like this: the wise man "definitely has the possession [*habitus*] of some things that the devotee [of wisdom] is only eager to have" (*TA* III.3.5). If so, Augustine wonders what it is he possesses—that is, if the Academics are correct in their view. Do they not say that the wise man knows nothing, and that wisdom only comes through suspension of assent (or consent)? If so, this seems to put paid to their thesis, and Alypius starts to show it in his faltering response. If he wants to hold on to this essential distinction, he will have to give content to the wise man's possession. Instead, he first tries to wriggle out of the problem by shifting responsibility onto the wise man himself. He starts speaking in terms of not what seems *to him* the case, but rather what seems to be *the wise man's* perspective. In short, he is suggesting his opinion does not matter. What matters is the wise man's perception of the matter, for he alone decides what his "wisdom" amounts to.

In response, Augustine implores him not to hide behind the wise man. It is time to stand up and do business with the question. "I'm not asking what it seems to you that *seems* to the wise man, but instead whether it seems to you that the wise man *knows* wisdom. You can, I take it, either affirm or deny it here and now." In short, this is no time for hiding in the shadows; at stake here is far more than intellectual victory. Either "deign [*digneris*] to answer the question I put to you," Augustine retorts, "rather than the one you put to yourself" (*TA* III.4.9). Or decide not to participate at all in debate. Once again, the verb *dignere* carries Christological weight, imploring him to "descend" from his lofty skeptical heights. If he does not step forward, Augustine is warning, the Academics will win by making losers of them both. Does he really want that?

A parable in book III sheds light on the predicament. Augustine tells of two travelers who are approaching the same place, and happen upon a crossroads that brings them to a stop. Consulting a local shepherd positioned nearby—likely a reference to Christ, scholars suggest—one traveler decides to trust the shepherd's advice, while the other stops to mock him for surrendering his assent. "The careful traveler laughs and ridicules the other for having assented so rapidly," Augustine comments. "While the other departs, he stands still at the fork in the road." As time passes by, though, the traveler feels foolish, until he is met by another man, "a well-dressed townsman riding on a horse," who persuades the careful traveler to continue the opposite way. It so happens however that this townsman is a "trickster," and misdirects the traveler toward the "out-of-the-way mountains." These mountains we met before in *The Happy Life* (Chapter 2, section "Locating Christ in the early works"). By recalling it here Augustine is drawing a connection between the sin of intellectual pride and Academic *epochē*. It is pride that refuses to come down from the mountain, and it is pride that refuses the humble advice of the shepherd. All told, the lesson he draws from this story is that no one escapes the risk of error in philosophy, not even the one who withholds his assent. In fact, "I think a man is in error not only when he follows the false path, but also when he's not following the true one" (*TA* III.15.34). This is another example of Augustine exploiting Cicero's mitigation of the Academic method.

We return now to Alypius at the proverbial crossroads. Augustine reiterates the question at hand: "Does it seem to *you* that the wise man knows wisdom, or doesn't it?" This time, Alypius takes a step toward response. Hesitantly, he finally comes around to saying yes: it does "seem to me that [the wise man] can [*potest*] know wisdom." In quick reply, Augustine issues yet another more pressing question, seizing on the *posse* in Alypius' response. "Therefore, I now ask you whether the wise man can be found [*possit inveneri*]. If he can, then he can know wisdom, and every question between us has been settled" (*TA* III.4.9). The argument boils down to one question, he suggests, a question buried deep within Cicero's calculative terms. Does Alypius harbor *hope* of finding the wise man; or does he lack such hope, and despair of finding wisdom? For Augustine, the possibility and probability of wisdom are covert expressions of the virtue of hope. It is hope, he argues, along with the faith that guides it, that carries true lovers to the end of their search: wisdom. The question is, does Alypius join Augustine at this point, or does he prefer standing still at the crossroads withholding assent?

Alypius still doubts the defeat of the Academics. After all, they do not need to respond to Augustine, and "I foresee that there is a strong defensive position reserved for [the Academics]: the suspension of assent." However, whereas Licentius took refuge in this position, Alypius seems ready to condemn it as pointless. All the constant shifting and protean arguing evidently leaves him feeling exhausted and despairing of the truth. It is then that he lights upon an insight into truth that sends the entire debate in a new, promising direction. Descending, so to speak, from the mountain of *epochē*, he offers up a prayer in the spirit of surrender: "May that divine spirit be present, and may he deign to show us [*demonstrare dignetur*] the truth that is of such importance to us! Then I'll also admit that the Academicians have been overcome even if they don't agree, although I think they will" (*TA* III.5.11).

A strange prayer indeed, but also a decisive one, as evidenced by how excited Augustine becomes after hearing it. His reasons for excitement include several received benefits. First, he is satisfied that the Academics agree with him: *if* the wise man can be found, he will be found to have wisdom. "'Who will show us the truth?' [*Sed quis eam demonstrabit*] they ask. I shall decline to get into a fight with them. It's enough for me that it is no longer plausible that the wise man knows nothing" (*TA* III.5.12). Moreover, that question is itself a significant breakthrough. It calls to mind Augustine's meditation on Psalm 4:6, the very Psalm he prayed the Manichees might voice, Romanianus in particular. Finally, Augustine celebrates the end of his debate with Alypius. The two agree on matters that pertain to religion, which is to say "human and divine matters combined with charity and good will" (*TA* III.6.13; citing Cicero, *De Amicitia*, 6.20). Alypius, it seems, has entered a place—the place of the moral self—in which love and goodwill, prayer and confession, hope and humility ground the search for truth. As a result, he surrenders his Academic position, *epochē*, and enters the place of security with Augustine.

* * * *

Finally, we reconnect with Augustine's final statement on the main false teaching of the Academic Skeptics: that none can find truth. Citing the skeptic Carneades as example—the one held responsible for mitigating skepticism—Augustine divulges why he ascribes a "far different view" to the Academics. Adopting the perspective of Carneades he writes:

> Have all of you [Academics] said that nothing whatsoever can be apprehended? At this point, Carneades woke up [*evigilavit*]—for none of the Academicians slept more lightly than he did—and looked about at the evidentness of things. So while talking to himself, as sometimes happens, I believe he said: "Well then, Carneades, are you going to say that you don't know whether you're a man or a bug?". (*TA* III.10.22)

Indeed, what Carneades had to do in that instant was the same thing Romanianus must do in this instant: stand upright, stir up the divine element within, and then begin to forge ahead with it in response to the voice of philosophy: asking, seeking, knocking. For Augustine, it was Carneades' reawakening to truth, "the evidentness of things," that initiated the discovery that the truth lies within (cf. *TA* III.18.40). "If you're asking me what *seems* to me so," he writes, "I think that the highest good of man is in the mind." Although he later would regret this way of putting the matter (*R* I.1.4), he would nevertheless maintain that our condition as "knowers" is that truth stands behind us, before us, and within us. It has come down to meet us in the humility of Christ.

> Yet the most subtle chain of reasoning would never call back to this intelligible world souls that have been blinded by the manifold shadows of error and rendered forgetful by the deepest filth of the body, had not God the Highest, moved by a certain compassion for the multitude, humbled and submitted the authority of the Divine Intellect even to a human body itself. Our souls, awakened [*excitatae*] not only by its precepts but also by its deeds, could return to themselves and regain their homeland without the strife of disputation. (*TA* III.19.42)

4

Escaping the Folly of Manichaeism

"True Religion"

In Chapter 3, we pursued a new reading of *The Academics*, framing it as an important first step to the moral self ("knowing"). In this chapter, we pursue the next step in this journey by exploring Augustine's argument against the Manichees. A natural point of connection is the treatise *True Religion* (AD 390–1). Alluded to already in *The Academics*, it is officially Augustine's follow-up with his friend Romanianus. In addition, it marks the high point of his early theological development: a moment when Augustine starts to draw his thoughts together. Its purpose as pledged is simple enough: liberate Romanianus from the shackles of Manichaeism, ease his surrender to the easy yoke of Christ (Van Fleteren *ATTA*, 864). Only this time, Augustine will direct his friend's steps to re-claim his position before God as a creature ("being").

In trying to raise up Romanianus to the creature, Augustine begins by summoning him *down* from the "mountain" (pride) and inviting him to enter "the place of security" (Chapter 2, section "Locating Christ in the early works"), namely confession and communion with the Church. Once again, it begins with the command to "ask, seek, knock." "Accordingly, let us make haste and walk while we still have the daylight, in case the dark should overtake us. Let us make haste to be delivered from the second death, in which there is no one who remembers God, and from hell, where nobody will confess to God" (*TR* 52.101, citing Jn. 12:35, Rv. 20:14, Ps. 6:5). Recall the situation of Romanianus at the time: a Manichee still clinging to the claim of enlightenment. As we saw in Chapter 3, the Manichees indulge pride by causing us to think that we have already "found some truth." This dissuades us from even seeking the truth, making us reject Christ's command altogether. Such pride fits a pattern tracing back to Genesis 3, a text Augustine begins to feature more in *True Religion*. He will again urge Romanianus to wake up, stand upright, and surrender himself fully to the pursuit of wisdom and truth. It is time for him to step out from hiding, he urges, and reckon with the truth of his condition in the world: a fallen, limited, but rational creature.

Turning inside out

Augustine is familiar with the Manichean trap. For nine years he suffered under the weight of its pretense (*TAB* 1.2), insulating his soul from exposure to the truth (*C* III.6.10). Having hid for so long in its comforting ways, indulging his appetite for corporeal images, he not only lost touch with "the way things are" but abandoned his position as a rational being. His displacement predisposed him to mock divine providence, holding God responsible for the chaos and disorder (the error of Adam; Chapter 2, section "Locating Adam in Genesis 3"). In *Expositions of the Psalms*, commenting again on Psalm 4:6, he excoriates the disposition of the typical Manichee:

> Many say, "Who has anything good to show us?" [Ps. 4:6/7]. This is the chatter [*sermo*], the daily questioning of all foolish and unjust people. Some of them crave peace and tranquility in this earthly life, yet do not find it because people are so tiresome. So blind are they to what is really happening that they have the cheek to find fault with the way things are [*ordinem rerum*]; wrapped up in their sense of their own goodness [*involuti meritis suis*], they think present times worse than the past. Or again, there are those who entertain doubts or despair of that future life which is promised to us. They often say, "Who knows if it's true? Who has ever come back from the dead to tell us about these things?" (*EP* 4.8).

It is convenient that this passage mentions two groups of people: those who "have the check to find fault with the way things are"— the Manichees. And those who "entertain doubts or despair of that future life"—the skeptically minded. Such is our journey from Chapter 3 to Chapter 4. Moreover, notice Augustine's different take on Psalm 4:6 (Chapter 3, section "1 Seeking and doubting"). It is no longer a Manichees's plea for illumination but a Manichees's slight against the goodness of God. A denouncement of "chatter" appears again in *True Religion:*

> There are many ways, however, that [the Christian religion] can be defended against chatterboxes and opened up to genuine seekers, with almighty God himself demonstrating its truths and helping persons of good will to behold and grasp them through the ministry of angels and of human beings of all sorts. (*TR* 10.20)

Such chatter inhibits one's search for the truth, replacing genuine enquiry with endless disputation. In the case of the Manichees who have walled themselves in, rejecting all authority (*auctoritas*) and elevating reason (*ratio*), they persist in cowardly hiding behind their monstrous self-conceit, indulging both them and their hearers "in their sense of their own goodness."

This posture not only puts them at odds with the truth; it also prevents them from seeking and reasoning toward truth. It is the same old story from Genesis 3—the Manichees representing both Adam and the serpent. In his early Genesis commentary Augustine writes: "[The] serpent signifies the various heretical poisons, and above all the one of these Manichees ... I am convinced, you see, that nothing is more manifestly foreshadowed in that serpent than this crew—or rather that it is he who is to be shunned in them." The serpent's deception leads to humanity's self-deception, which corrupts the interior nature of the intellect and heart. "[I]t was through pride that the sin was put across," making Adam and Eve "too fond of their own power ... wishing to be God's equals ... and so forfeit[ing] what they had received, while they had wanted to grab what they had not received." Just as Adam and Eve suffered the effect of displacement, enticed by the serpent's promise to *be like Gods* (Gn. 3:5), so Augustine also suffered the effect of displacement, having once believed the Manichees that he *is* God. The cause in both cases was the sin of human pride, which infests the root and branch of Manichean devotion: "who else says it more than these people, striving with their proud nonsense to lead others into the same kind of pride, and affirming that the soul is by nature what God is?" (*GRM* II.35.38).

In turning from God, Adam turned to himself, and chose to delight in his own *received* goodness and powers. "[I]f the soul turns to itself [*ad seipsam*] with its back to God and wants to enjoy its own power without any reference to God, it swells up with pride, which is *the starting point of all sin* (Sir. 10:13)" (*GRM* II.9.12). Turning away, Adam gloried in his own created nature, exchanging God's truth for the lie of the serpent. The truth he exchanged is the truth of his creatureliness, resulting in his displacement from that creaturely position, "forfeiting what [he] had received ...." Now, it is only by recovering that creatureliness that Romanianus can begin restoring himself to himself. If Adam turned inward away from the truth, Romanianus must turn inward and upward to the truth; and to do so, he must begin by heeding the outward call of God.

* * * *

Turning back to God is a journey of desire, beginning with the slightest inclination toward the truth. But when the resistance is too strong and the pride too inflated, it is better not to engage than to try to win the argument. In *The Advantage of Believing*, Augustine remarks that there are heretics and those who believe the heretics, and "These two things ... are not the same at all." The heretic, he says, is "the author of false and novel views," and may promote his views "for the sake of some temporal gain." Whereas the one who believes them is mistaken but a victim, "seduced by a veneer of truth and devotion" (*TAB* 1.1). The distinction is intended as a challenge to the reader: how will you respond to the call to seek the truth?

In Chapter 2, we saw Augustine criticize the Manichees for not seeking truth "with reverent inquiry." In *The Catholic Way of Life*, another early moral treatise, he states his purpose is to help the Manichees "desire the light of Christian faith," but that this will only happen "if they are willing to wake up [*evigilare*] and set aside their stubborn dreams" (*TCWL* I.1.2). Now, addressing Romanianus in *True Religion*, he issues a stern statement on how to begin: "Pay pious and diligent attention, therefore, to what follows, as best you can. People like that, after all, are the ones to whom God gives a helping hand" (*TR* 10.20; cf. *R* I.13.4). God resists the proud but gives grace to the humble (Prov. 3:34). In this case, the humble are lovers on a quest, and lovers on a quest seek the truth with devotion. As for heretics, they are there as a gift from divine providence, "prodding [*excitando*] fleshly-minded Catholics into seeking the truth and spiritual ones into opening up its riches" (*TR* 10.20). If the Academics could not wake Romanianus to the truth, perhaps the Manichees can prove more "useful" to that end (cf. *TR* 8.15).

Augustine recalls his mindset from his Manichean days. What attracted him then, he explains to Honoratus in *The Advantage of Believing*, was how the Manichees "declared with awesome authority, quite removed from pure and simple reasoning, that if any persons chose to listen to them they would turn them to God and free them from all error." Simply put, they promised to teach him the truth through argument, an offer that proved attractive to "a young man yearning for the truth and made proud and outspoken by the debates in the classes of certain scholars …" (*TAB* 1.2). Now in a position to see the folly of his ways, he is set upon exposing it in his former co-religionists. That folly includes an outright rejection of authority and an inward devotion to the powers of reason.

"Authority demands faith and paves the way to use reason. Reason leads on to understanding and knowledge, although reason is not entirely wanting in authority, when one considers who precisely has to be believed, and certainly the Truth itself, once perspicuously known, has supreme authority (*TR* 24.45). For Augustine, to reason is to rely on authority, above all the authority of the transcendent Truth. As Ryan Topping puts it, "Reason is a muscle that needs to be exercised in relation to concrete authorities" (Topping 2012: 187). Authority gives ground for reason to occur, for reason cannot stand on its own two feet. It cannot be the *sole* launching point of enquiry (Rist 2001: 27), which is *not* to say that reason has no power or utility. To the contrary, reason matures in response to authority and gains its firm footing in allegiance to the Truth. The question always facing it is which authority to trust; that is, assuming it first ask, seeks, knocks.

The function of authority is essential to Augustine and provides a notable contrast to the modern way of reason. In *The Advantage of Believing*, he recalls his past struggle to gain a proper view of the role and scope of reason.

> Often it seemed to me that [the truth] could not be found, and I turned the great flood of my thoughts to the opinions of the academics. Often, as best I could, I would look again at the human mind, so lively, so discerning, so perceptive, and I would think that the truth could not lie hidden unless the way to search for it lay hidden and that that way had itself to be obtained from some divine authority. It only remained to find out what authority that was, since among all their disagreements everyone promised to provide it. (*TAB* 8.20)

As we saw in Chapter 3, his solution to the problem is to trust himself completely to the authority of Christ. This was a conclusion he arrived at eventually after realizing that authority is always part of human reasoning; not even the Skeptics can avoid it entirely, as Cicero exhibited through his mitigated skepticism (Chapter 3, section "Seeking, not finding"). Yet, what does he mean by authority and "divine authority"? He does not mean authority in the authoritarian sense; that is not authority but the abuse of authority (O'Donovan 2002: 69, 70). Augustine does not doubt such abuse can occur, but nor does he think it *cancels out* our need for authority. Instead, it merely sharpens the dilemma we all face: Which authority can we trust? On what basis can we determine that?

If suspicion of all authority leaves us standing at the crossroads (skepticism) and reason alone is a self-gratifying folly (rationalism), the answer Augustine arrives at is not to reject reason, but to ground it in a community bound by charity and goodwill, that is, true philosophy. If this community had its start in the Cassiciacum context, reaching its high point in Alypius' prayer in *The Academics* (Chapter 3, "Seeking as praying"), it will continue as Augustine turns his eye to the Manichees and appeals on behalf of those "hearers" (not heretics) he calls friends.

His first appeal comes in *The Catholic Way of Life*. In this treatise he faces an immediate problem: the Manichees do not accept the claims of authority. Instead, in violation of the "natural order" [*ordo naturae*] they demand that all arguments make their case through reason. In response, Augustine notes that this order serves human interests. It supports our weakness, protects us from pride (and despair), and leads "the wavering eye into the light of the truth." Since, however, the Manichees refuse this order (out of pride, of course), they erect a major obstacle to reasoning together. If they will not step down to where Catholics reside—which is where they reside too—then they give him no choice but to act as the fool. To meet the Manichees where they claim to reside, Augustine will suspend the natural order and pursue truth through reason. Notably, to justify deploying this "defective manner of arguing," he presents himself as imitating the example of Christ. "For I find delight in imitating, as much as I can, the gentleness of my Lord Jesus Christ, who clothed himself even with the evil of death of which he wanted to strip us" (*TCWL* I.2.3).

From there, he launches an eudaemonist argument that hinges on acknowledging that the self is a lover; that is, a seeker who desires the happy life. "Let us, then, investigate by reason how a human being ought to live" (*TCWL* I.2.4). To begin, says Augustine, we must agree on one thing. We must agree that our desire is to live a happy life. To deny this desire is not an option, he implies, but a condition for conducting this discussion altogether. Why? The same reason it was established as a condition in *The Academics*: firstly it demonstrates a participant's "good will" [*bona voluntas*], not denying the obvious that all desire happiness; and secondly it establishes a fundamental axiom prior to the dictates of reason and authority: the self-evident "first principle" of desire for happiness (Marion 2012: 87), without which *no lover* can address the human good. This desire is self-evident to any sober-minded lover, to anyone not bent on quarreling for its own sake. Securing this confession is for Augustine half the battle: simply because it locates us (the reader) in a specific disposition that is *not* the disposition of the cold-blooded rationalist or high-minded heretic. Indeed, it sets us up to discover *through* reason that reason *by itself* cannot attain the happy life.

Let us summarize how Augustine brings about this discovery. Having secured our agreement that we desire the happy life, he proposes that our search is for the highest good of reality, the *summum bonum*. For every attempt at securing this life through the body, and every attempt at securing this life through the soul, ultimately suffers either decay or the change of opinion, leaving us always fearing the eventual loss of our happiness. If neither body nor soul can secure for us happiness, via permanence and control

(Wetzel 1992: 75), then our good must lie in something beyond body and soul: a spiritual good. This good, says Augustine, is in fact the *summum bonum*: and all religious people do not hesitate to call this God (he sets aside atheists). The real question then is how to attain the *summum bonum*. Surely it is the mind not the body that attains it, yet the mind seems to struggle upon making the ascent. Even if it catches a glimpse of God's light, the mind's reason falls away "not by choice but out of fatigue," betraying its weakness as the Manichees were warned. That is why reason needs assistance in its quest: it cannot find God on its own presumed strength, moral and intellectual, but first must grow stronger in virtue and wisdom. To do so it must travel down the way of authority, having recourse "to the directives of those who probably were wise. Reason could be brought to this point [alone]" (*TCWL* I.7.11). In this way reason discovers, *if it is true to its object,* that the only reasonable path is the path of authority.

The onus is on reason to be true to its object; that is, if reason truly seeks to find the supreme good, it will discover that this good places demands on the seeker. These demands include training in a virtuous life: the good is not indifferent to the moral state of humanity. If, then, the Manichees have made it this far (and Augustine has his doubts), they will begin to ask not whether but *which* authority to trust. Why not the authority that reaches down to *them*, responding to their weakness and supporting their search? Augustine exclaims, "What more could have been done on behalf of our salvation? What can be said to be more beneficent, what can be said to be more generous than divine providence?" (*TCWL* I.7.12). Assuming the Manichees are now wearied by hunger (Chapter 3, section "Seeking and doubting") they might cease all this nonsense about reason *or* authority, and instead come to reckon with their real limitations: not to mention the increased weight of their desire for truth. As Augustine later clarifies, his goal at this point is *not* "that you may now understand these [divine] ideas, for that is not possible, but ... that you may desire [*cupiatis*] to understand them at some point" (*TCWL* I.17.31).

* * * *

The goal of Augustine's treatise, as the goal of all his writings, is to awaken deep desires for the truth of which he speaks. This includes showing reason the way of authority, calling the Manichees to come down from their arrogance. Or to change the metaphor, it is to unwrap the Manichees, turning them "inside out" to receive the gifts of God. If this began with *The Academics*, it now continues with *True Religion*; we turn there now.

Armed with a fuller set of biblical and theological arguments, *True Religion* locates the soul in an intense moral struggle. The soul, Augustine writes, is like a warrior "engaged in the stadium of human life." It must beat "those greedy desires" to attain the unchangeable Wisdom. Linking this battle to Genesis 3 Augustine highlights the background of Adam's displacement. "[Adam] ignored [God's] command, you see, his telling: 'Eat this, don't eat that.' So then he is dragged off to punishment, because by loving low things he is assigned his place among the lowest, lacking all his pleasures, enduring all his pains" (*TR* 12.23). Adam not only serves as the backstory to humanity, but also the template for a renewed human nature. "God's inexpressible mercy comes to the rescue both of individual and of the whole human race by means of a creature subject to change and yet obedient to divine laws, *to remind the soul* of its primal and perfect nature" (*TR* 10.19, emphasis added). Adam's nature, vitiated through pride and through sin, is the same nature humans are being summoned to recover. Who is this "creature subject to change" [*per creaturam mutabilem*]? In this case, Augustine is referring to Christ.

For Augustine, Christ's mission was to serve as a reminder (*admonitio*) as well as provide humans with a model of obedience. "So the whole of his life on earth, then, as lived by the man he had the goodness to take to himself, was a lesson in morals. His resurrection from the dead, however, was a sufficient indication that no part of human nature is lost ..." (*TR* 16.32; 55.110). In short, Christ came as an example to imitate (Cameron 2012: 122). He assists in the recovery and restoration of human nature, demonstrating to humans how to reclaim Adam's place. It is here, in the distinction between Creator and creature, that Romanianus finds his way to the one true religion: "Let us then but avoid *serving the creature rather than the creator*, and *becoming vain in our thoughts* (Rom. 1:25.21), and religion is all it should be" (*TR* 10.19).

Not surprisingly, these claims have raised a few readers' eyebrows for what they seem to omit in the way of orthodox Christology. The argument put forward most recently by Brian Dobell—reviving the century-old thesis of Lord Prosper Alfaric (Chapter 2, section "Locating Christ in the early works")—is that Augustine at this time espoused a Photinian Christology that he did not correct until many years later (even up to AD 395). Instead for him, Jesus Christ was a man inspired by God (or the "Virtue of God and the Wisdom of God"), and therefore *not* God come down in the flesh. He did not atone for our sins on the cross (see Dewart 1984 for Augustine's early view of the cross), and he does not offer us himself in the sacrament. To the contrary, says Dobell, Christ appears in his person as "an eminent wise man: he has been assumed by the Virtue and Wisdom of God, and he serves as an intermediary between the foolishness and viciousness of man and the Virtue and Wisdom of God." And "with respect to his work, Christ is an outstanding example of virtue: his example is manifest in such miracles as his virgin birth, and his death and resurrection. These miracles attest to his authority, and the soul of the fool may be purified by imitating his example" (Dobell 2009: 65, 66). Indeed, at no point before or in *True Religion* (or even some time after) does Augustine spell out any clearer orthodox Christology. Rather, as he acknowledges in *Confessions* book VII (on Dobell's reading), he appears to have subscribed to the Photinian heresy in which Christ is not God but a divinized human being, "a creature subject to change."

At the very least, there is no reason to dispute Dobell's claim that Augustine fails to dispel all rumors about his Christology. If we ask whether Christ is the savior in his works, or merely shows others how to be their own saviors (through obedience, imitation, etc.), we may certainly find evidence to suggest the latter is true, without conclusively proving Augustine's views were heretical. In fact, this effort to pin down Augustine brings its own set of assumptions to Augustine's early works. The idea that Augustine had a worked-out Christology sets in motion an investigation to compile the evidence; and yet, if this evidence does not cohere all that well, that may be because Augustine did not seek such coherence. Instead, allowing Christ to "show up" where he would, he sought to prepare readers to receive and confess him. Of course, it does matter if they confess the wrong views. If Christ is *only* a reminder of our "primal and perfect nature," that would make him a mere placeholder among other effective placeholders. Similarly, if Christ is only an example to imitate, his work would succeed only in pointing the way, rather than offering us salvation in himself (Jn. 14:6). At the same time, that Christ would achieve *this much* is by no means nothing, but contributes to salvation. It would mean Christ positions us to seek and find the truth, making us worthy and "fit" [*idonea*] to receive illumination. If that is how Augustine views Christ in this work, then depending on how accommodating we are toward his journey (or, he might say, charitable) we can still learn something from the progress he makes.

Where does Augustine want us to arrive? "If we cling to the eternal creator, we too are bound to be affected by eternity" (*TR* 10.19). To become this kind of lover, as we learned in *The Catholic Way of Life*, requires training in virtue in obedience to authority. In *True Religion* he describes it as "a way of life accommodated to the divine commandments [that] will purge the mind and make it capable of grasping spiritual realities ..." (*TR* 7.13). These commandments essentially center on the double love command (Mt. 22), and in this, Augustine is unique among early Christian moralists (O'Donovan 1980; Canning 1993). Subordinating the four virtues to the love of God and neighbor (O'Donovan 1994: 223), he will single out Jesus Christ, "the Virtue of God and the Wisdom of God" (*TCWL* I.13.22; correcting Teske's translation of *virtus*), as the source by which souls become formed and reformed. The means of (re-)formation is the love of God the Father, inspired by the Spirit, working together with the Son; as he puts it in *The Catholic Way of Life*, "Love, then, will see to it that we are conformed to God and, having been conformed and configured by him and cut off from this world, that we are not confused with the things that ought to be subject to us. But this is done by the Holy Spirit" (*TCWL* I.13.23). He repeats the Trinitarian formula several times in this work (see Gerber 2012: 128–140), developing it further in *True Religion*. On the Form of Christ he writes,

> And so the Son is rightly said to be *from* [God], everything else to be *through* [the Word]. He came forth, you see, as the form or shape of all things, supremely achieving the one, from whom he is, so that all other things that are, insofar as they are like the One, become so through that form or shape. (*TR* 43.81; cf. Harrison 2006: 104ff)

In these statements, he identifies Christ's mission on earth as "*a program of spiritual instruction that would communicate God's form* and so refurbish the divine image within the human race" (Cameron 2012: 118, emphasis original). And with that, we can see why he exhorts Romanianus to wake up, stand up, and take responsibility for his reason; that is where God deigns to meet him in Christ. "Let us walk while we have the light of day, that is, while we can still make use of reason, so that being converted and turned towards God by his Word, which is the true light, we may deserve to be enlightened, lest the dark overtake us" (*TR* 42.79).

How does Christ form souls in virtue and wisdom? At least in two ways: first, by issuing moral commands; second, by uniting Scripture's "message" in himself. For Augustine, by believing in the unity of Scripture, Old and New Testaments, one progresses even further to a reformed human nature. Such faith is found lacking in the listless Manichees whose sole motive in reading amounts to "captious fault-finding." Their inability or unwillingness to perceive Scripture's unity leads to blindness to the unity of the way things are. Whereas to those set on fire by love of truth and wisdom, unity is a reality they rejoice to discover. All the pleas Augustine issues to *wake up* and *pay attention* serve the purpose of delivering Manichees to love of unity (cf. *OO* II.18.48). The motivation in calling them to attend to the Scriptures is the conviction that reading can be a site of salvation (Stock 2010: 35–39), the place where God meets them and orders their souls. Ultimately, it is the place where God calls out "Where are you?" and receives either a response or a failure to respond, this response hinging on how well we care for our souls. "Hence, if you have any humanity in your heart, if you care about yourselves, seek rather with diligence and piety the sense in which those things [in Scripture] are said. Seek, you poor wretches" (*TCWL* I.10.17).

In the end, it is the call to attend to Christ himself that tests the lover's motives and goodwill toward the truth.

> Listen to Christ himself; listen, I repeat, to *Christ*; listen to *the wisdom of God* (1 Cor. 1:24). He says, *The whole law and all the prophets depend on these two commandments*. With your most impudent stubbornness, what can you say about this passage? That Christ did not say this? These words of his are written in the gospel … The worshipers of idols, who hate even the name of Christ, have never dared to say this against those scriptures. (*TCWL* I.29.60)

There are consequences in questioning Christ's words, Augustine warns, for it places all ancient words in doubt, including the Manichees'. Yet, if the Manichees will not heed the command of Christ, ask, seek, knock (*TCWL* I.17.31, I.18.34), what point is there debating what Christ said or did not say?

Turning outside in

In *True Religion*, Augustine seeks to deliver Romanianus to the authority of Christ. By giving him a model of true virtue and wisdom (action and contemplation) Christ positions Romanianus to use reason to good effect. What bridges the gap between authority and reason is Romanianus' obedience to the command of Christ in Matthew 7. Moreover, by learning to love order and unity, and by affirming divine providence and its care for the soul (*TCWL* I.6.10; *TR* 7.13), Romanianus gains a foothold in the order of reality in preparation for examining and transcending that reality. In this section, then, we embark on Augustine's second step to preparing Romanianus to embrace the true religion. We analyze his method of turning inward to the soul to evaluate the innate powers and resources of human reason: "that divine element within."

* * * *

Augustine states that the soul "is being summoned ... to stillness, that is, not to set its heart on things which you cannot set your heart on without hard labor" (*TR* 35.65). He expounds on this stillness in *Expositions of the Psalms*. "*When I was hard beset you led me into spacious freedom* [Ps. 4:2]; that is, from the cramped conditions of sorrow you have led me into the broad open fields of joy and gladness." Referencing his favorite verse Romans 5:5, he writes our "heart does not live in a poky little room," but instead enjoys "convers[ing] inwardly" through the Spirit "poured into our hearts already" (*EP* 4.2). Evidently, turning inward is not an isolating practice, at least not when the soul sets its sight upon God. Expanding the heart chambers through the gift and grace of God, turning inward disposes the soul to acknowledge God's presence. "You were more intimately present to me than my innermost being, and higher than the highest peak of my spirit" (*C* III.6.10). God summons creatures to be still in his presence, to re-open channels for divine-human communication. We learn in this place how to hear God's voice, which enables us to reclaim our role in God's world. "And that is why, if the rational soul serves her creator, by whom she has been made and through whom she has been made and to whom she has been made, all other things will serve her" (*TR* 44.82). The challenge is in becoming that obedient rational soul; this is what Augustine calls, drawing on Paul, the "interior person" [*interior homo*], and elsewhere, drawing on Genesis, the image and likeness of God.

In a reflection on Psalm 4:7, "The light of your countenance is stamped on us, O Lord," he will bring the two together in the following way. First the image of God:

> This light is the complete and true good of humankind; it is not seen with the eyes but with the mind. The psalmist's phrase, *stamped upon us*, suggests a coin stamped with the king's picture. For the human individual has been made in God's image and likeness [*ad imaginem et similitudinem*], something which each has corrupted by sinning.

Then, expounding on Psalm 4:8, "You have given joy in my heart," he comments:

> Joy, therefore, is not to be sought outside oneself, by those who, still heavy in heart, love emptiness and chase falsehood [Ps. 4:3]. Rather, it is to be sought within [*intus*], where the light of God's face is stamped. For Christ dwells in the inner person [*interiore homine*], as the apostle says [Eph. 3:17]; and to Christ belongs the capacity to see the truth, for he said, *I am the truth* [Jn. 14:6]. (*EP* 4.8)

Christ is involved in our capacity to see the truth. He is the Teacher who inwardly illuminates the soul, and the Form by which intellect achieves its capacity. He is further said to dwell somewhere "in" the inner person, which is a metaphor a reader could take in any number of directions. What does Augustine mean by "in" and "inside"?

Evidently, he does not mean where the Manichees are, wrapped up in a sense of their own goodness and powers. Augustine's inside is not cramped, closed off, but poised in a stillness full of joy and with room to roam. The metaphor however is elusive in its meaning, and to some scholars creates more problems than solutions (Cary 2000). It is here that we propose a new account of interiority by framing it as a strategy of reclaiming the moral self. In our view, what Augustine increasingly means by "inside" is a conscientious awareness of oneself before God. This awareness includes realizing the image of God within—or rather, the image to which humans are being converted, *ad imaginem et similitudinem Dei*—as well as confessing the origin and destiny of human being, knowing, and willing. Most of all, it involves an increasing recognition of the weight of human love for what is Goodness-Itself: in another vein, for the Truth by whom all things are true, and the Form through whom and in whom all things receive form.

To this end, the soul must first come to terms with itself, opening a conversation with its own rational powers. Augustine calls this the act of "soliloquy" [*soliloquium*], a term and a genre he apparently invented (Stock 2010). As Brian Stock observes, Augustine's inner dialogue has the function of expanding the self's knowledge of itself. As "spiritual exercises" in the philosophical mode (Stock 2010: 18ff), it serves to awaken and illumine the self (or the mind, or reason) to realities buried deep within the self's origin and nature. One such reality already mentioned is desire for happiness (Stock 2010: 45, 46). A first principle of the self's self-involvement with the world, desire for happiness opens a window onto the place of the self. It constitutes that place as an animating energy that motivates the self, haunts and displaces it, while disposing it to experience and encounter the world not as an assemblage of randomly arranged parts—"disordered" to Manichees, "disenchanted" to moderns—but as a providentially ordered and communicative whole displaying intelligibility as an *unum in diversis*, a universe (OO I.1.1–4). Through soliloquy, then, one calls up desire to try and make sense of its relation to the whole. To do this, however, also requires creating "space," and more specifically the appropriate "distance" between the world and the self.

To create this distance between the world and the self—what Augustine describes as standing up and out in the crowd—one begins to "put a question" to the order of the world, thereupon distinguishing and reclaiming one's location. For, ontologically speaking, we are a particular sort of creature: not rocks or trees, plants or animals, even though we share with each "being" [*esse*] and "living" [*vivere*]. We also have the capacity of intelligence or "understanding" (*intellegere*), a trait that marks us out as being created to the divine image and likeness. As beings, then, who are capable of thought and reflection, we also possess an ability to act as we wish. For Augustine, this singles out our being-in-the-world as not only ontologically but morally distinct, endowing our nature with both freedom and responsibility; but this is where things start to go wrong for humanity. In *True Religion*, the moral dimension of the self-in-the-world starts to acquire greater significance in the sphere of salvation. It is clarified that the problem with the self-in-the-world is not the world we inhabit, but rather how we live in it. For example, Augustine invites us to put a question to the body, but immediately stresses that the body is not the source of the problem. Rather, it is how we take pleasure in the body, investing it with meaning beyond the meaning it has.

> [E]ven with these pleasures of the body we find that the reason for disdaining them is not that the nature of the body is something bad but that it is shameful to wallow in the love of this last and lowest of good things when you have been granted the privilege of cleaving to and enjoying the first and highest. (*TR* 48.53)

However, should we attend more closely to the body, we will discover in the body a sign or "hint" of the blessed life (*TR* 45.84). This allows us to recover our location before God, neither giving too high or too low a self-estimate. "And to think that [Adam] would only have submissively to imitate God by living according to his commandments, and he would have all the other things made subject to him and would not sink to such baseness as to be afraid of that beastie [the serpent] who wants to have humanity at his beck and call!" (*TR* 45.84).

At the same time, the self's trajectory on and up through creation—even to the point of "disdaining" bodily attachments—throws into question how substantial Augustine's view of creation is, as well as calls to mind the allegations against his Christology. Simply put, creation is a signifier of eternity, rather than an object of attention in itself. The beauty it displays, the goodness it manifests, lack the integrity of fully concretized realities. As Carol Harrison remarks, beauty in this period is "defined as a mathematical, rational, abstract proposition, concretized in a fragmentary way in created reality, which finds its true home in the mind, intellect, and reason, above which dwells its eternal archetype ..." (Harrison 1992: 31). On the other hand, what motivates this judgment by Augustine are enduring concerns about idolatrous worship. By creating affective distance between body and soul, he takes a strong line against the mind's self-abasement through investing its desires in the things of this world. At the same time, such a line elicits certain moral conclusions that Augustine later regrets as being improperly Christian (see below). The general trend in his thinking at this point is to view the category "good" as a reality scaling upward, partially "realized" in the transience of creation. The alternative view and, indeed, his more mature one, does not disdain the good of creation as good in itself: located *in* creation as an embodied reality ("incarnated"). In fact, herein lurks one of the major temptations to depicting the moral life as a journey back to God. To declare created objects as both beautiful and good, only then to reveal that "all the time it is really God lurking behind these objects" (O'Donovan 1994: 123), is to rob those objects of not only their (given) integrity, but also their (given) authority to summon us to action. Not to sidestep or mitigate the force of this challenge, we have observed already how, by emphasizing the role of authority, Augustine is well positioned to make the adjustment.

In any event, up against the dogged rationalism of Manichaeism, Augustine clearly wishes to bring this inner dialogue to a point: a reckoning, so to speak, with the divine truth itself, not to be identified with any "thing" in this world. Instead, he wants a thinker with a view beyond the world. "O obstinate souls, give me someone who can see, without imaging any flesh-bound things seen ... Give me not someone who argues, not someone who wishes to seem to see what he does not see." Indeed, he wants someone who will "stand up against [*resistat*] the senses of the flesh ... human custom ... human praise," and who "*will be sorry on his bed* (Ps. 4:4), who *will rectify his spirit* (Ps. 77:6), who will not *love vanities and go in search of lies* (Ps. 4:2)" (*TR* 34.64). In other words, not a thinker who is proud in his thoughts, but a thinker whose thinking is being called into question. This is the next step in Augustine's inward turn.

* * * *

Augustine's interest in the nature and capacity of reason takes off right away in the Cassiciacum period. During this time, he launches an investigation into reason that praises not only its power but its proximity to divinity. As a matter of fact Phillip Cary, in a close reading of *Soliloquies* (AD 386), makes the case that Augustine identifies reason as divine, and also by implication the soul as divine. Not only that, by arguing that the soul is divine he inadvertently elevates the soul above the Truth—all this to prove that the soul is immortal (Cary 2000: 95–104). While the details of Cary's reading cannot occupy us here, let us pause briefly to comment on Augustine's possible objective.

First of all, it is notable that despite his careful analysis, Cary never mentions Augustine's account of the image of God. To be sure, Augustine himself only mentions it in passing (cf. *TS* I.1.4), but that does not mean he did not apply it at the time, as we demonstrated in Chapter 3. If he did apply it then, how does that clarify his objective? Of course, he could have viewed the image of God as divine, or even failed to read it as a meaningful distinction. Better yet—this in keeping with his sensitivity to pride—he may have approached the image of God as a fraught field of enquiry; a perilous venture on a complicated question. He addresses such a danger a year or two later in *The Catholic Way of Life*. Declaring God more excellent than the soul, he explains there is a danger in the soul's proximity to God. The soul, being "counted among invisible and intelligible things ... might by pride [*superbia*] fall away from him to whom it should be united by love." And, though the soul rightly desires to become like God,

> if it becomes very close to him through that subjection by which it becomes like him, the audacity by which it wants to be more like him [*audacia qua vult esse similior*] must become far removed from it. This is the audacity by which it refuses to obey the laws of God when it wants to be in its own power, as God is. (*TCWL* I.12.20)

Clearly, this is echoing Genesis 3 in which Adam abuses the image by trying to transcend it. The "audacity" by which Adam sought to seize divine likeness (that is, equality with God) also lurks in the biblical command to become like God. Perhaps Augustine observed this danger at Cassiciacum and was consequently struggling to articulate the nature of the soul.

Furthermore, at the conclusion of his dialogue in *Soliloquies*, Augustine appears to change course on the soul's relation to Truth. He begins to relate the Truth to the soul through conversion, rather than attempt to ground the Truth in the soul. Addressing the influence of corporeal images on the soul, Augustine's interlocutor *Ratio* claims that in order to find the Truth (which is incorporeal), the soul must gaze "fully and completely at the face of truth [*faciem veritatis*], whose splendor shines faintly in those [liberal] arts." Then, in explicating the power of judgment, *Ratio* claims that "the inner mind [*mens interior*], which wishes to see what is true, turns [*convertat*] rather, if it can, toward that according to which it judges all these squares are true" (*S* II.20.35). This is an oblique reference to Christ "the visage of philosophy" [*facies philosophiae*] (*TA* II.3.7), for as Truth, Christ dwells within and illuminates the soul. Elsewhere, Augustine calls Christ "the discipline of disciplines" (*L* 11.4) and even gives dialectic the mission of Christ. "[Dialectic] teaches both how to learn and how to teach. In it, reason exhibits itself to itself .... It knows what knowledge is; and by itself it not only wishes to make men learned, but also can make them so" (*OO* II.13.38). Again, none of this proves Cary's reading is wrong, but it does point the way to Augustine's later account (as we shall see in a moment).

However, the greater challenge Cary levels against Augustine is centered on his practice of turning inward to the soul: a practice with both ontological and moral implications. Ontologically, by privileging the "interior" realm—a realm of incorporeal ideas and realities—Augustine lowers our estimation of the "external" corporeal realm—the realm where Christ came to dwell in the flesh (Cary 2008). Obviously, if Augustine lacks a developed Christology this result is not accidental but precisely intended. However, it also has moral implications insofar as it privileges the interior life over the exterior. By focusing on the inside instead of the outside, Augustine seems to discourage moral encounters with the world. His starting point for reckoning with our place in the world ends up erecting a barrier between different interior lives, isolating and concealing each life from the other, and creating many problems in their ability to relate—a theme most familiar to the modern moral discourse (see Introduction; see also Cary 1996). At the extreme, this interiority gives rise to the judgment—most famously set forth and applied in *The City of God*—that we cannot know for certain the intentions of another, not even a friend's, which means we cannot secure peace in any society on this earth. "And even peace is a doubtful good, since we do not know the hearts of those with whom we wish to maintain peace, and even if we could know them today, we should not know what they might be like tomorrow" (*TCG* XIX.5; cf. *FU* 1–3.5).

If turning inward has the effect of creating dissension not concord, isolating the self from the world and the other (if not *the* Other), it would work against the goal Augustine sets for Romanianus, which is to regain his freedom under the easy yoke of Christ, while unwrapping the pretenses that stifle his development. However, by examining the next step in interiority we can draw some different conclusions about the goal of the practice.

Turning inside up

Turning inward is a method of self-examination that begins by putting a question to the outside world. Then, turning that question onto the mind that questioned, it facilitates the re-discovering of the mind's capacity to reason. Now the mind standing upright, distinguished from creation, starts to ponder its condition and desires in creation. It began by catching a glimpse of creation's order, beauty, and goodness, and even marveled at the degree to which it manifests those things. However, it cannot stop there, and must not stop there, given the weight of its desire is to know the way things are. In the third and final move, the mind turns inside up, opening "the eye of the mind" (*TR* 35.65) to the light from above: Truth itself. As we shall see, the result is not only intellectual discovery, but also a new opening to the place of the moral self.

* * * *

In *The Catholic Way of Life*, the soul's renovation unfolds within a scripturally framed Trinitarian structure. Beginning with God the Father, to whom we "ought to be subject" (*TCWL* I.16.25), it transitions to God the Son who shapes us and teaches us, and then to the Spirit who inspires our journey. With the Father, the emphasis is on adherence through love (Ps. 72:78), for God is the end for which the soul longs and strives. With the Son, the focus is on "activity" and "teaching" corresponding to the "virtue and wisdom of God." At this stage, Augustine lingers over the role played by Christ in preparing us to love God with sobriety and justice. "I do not know what I should compare to these two, that is, to the effectiveness of action and the sobriety of contemplation, which the [virtue] of God and the wisdom of God, that is, the Son of God, *gives* to those who love him" (*TCWL* I.16.28; emphasis added). What Christ gives is our positioning in the love of God the Father, a positioning made possible by obedience to Christ. Moreover, Augustine cites for the first time his favorite verse, Romans 5:5, combining it with other Pauline verses and the Psalms.

> Paul says, The love of God has been poured out in our hearts through the Holy Spirit who has been given to us (Rom. 5:5). The prophet says, For the Holy Spirit of discipline will banish deceit (Wis. 1:5). For, where there is deceit, there is no love. Paul says that we are becoming conformed to the image of the Son of God [Rom. 8:29]. The prophet says, The light of your countenance, O Lord, has been impressed upon us. (Ps. 4:7)

By joining Psalm 4:7 to Romans 8:29, he gestures to his new view of the soul's renovation: formation in Christ through the Spirit's gift of love (Gerber 2012: 145–150). Though not yet identifying the Spirit *with* love, he is already anticipating that discovery here, in addition to already linking the divine image to Christ. Two more statements bear this out: "Love, then, will see to it that we are conformed to God and, having been conformed and configured by him and cut off from this world, that we are not confused with the things that ought to be subject to us. But this is done by the Holy Spirit" (*TCWL* I.13.23). "For the simple and pure love of God, which is especially seen in one's way of life, brings [understanding] about …. Once it has been breathed into us by the Holy Spirit [Rom. 5:5], it leads us to the Son, that is, to the wisdom of God, through whom the Father himself comes to be known" (*TCWL* I.17.31).

Then in *True Religion*, Augustine narrows his focus to how Christ models for us the true path to redemption. Invoking the "triple temptation" of 1 John 2:15–16—sins of the flesh (*cupditas*), sins of the eyes (*curiositas*), secular ambition (*superbia*)—he shows how Christ overcame these sins in the desert (Mt. 4) by rejecting

Satan's offers to abandon obedience. He sums up the lesson in the following way:

> those who feed inwardly on the word of God do not seek pleasure in this desert [*cupiditas*]; those who submit to the one God alone do not seek things to boast about on the mountain, that is on earthly achievement [*superbia*]; while those who cleave to the eternal spectacle of unchanging Truth do not hurl themselves down by means of the summit of this body, that is of these eyes, to acquire knowledge of the lower things of time [*curiositas*]. (*TR* 38.71; cf. *GRM* II.25.40)

In each case, Christ effectively defeats the temptation by directing his love to the one true God; this is precisely what reason must do now to avoid pointlessly worshiping its creaturely power. In this way, Christ holds the creature's place before God.

If religion stands or falls on the Creator-creature distinction, Augustine's goal is to establish that distinction through confession. In talking through the matter with his friend Romanianus he explains explain how the soul, despite its power, cannot find its own principle and foundation in itself. Capable of sitting in judgment over reality and even the senses that "report" on reality, the rational soul does not make true judgments "of its own accord," but only in accord with "some art or discipline or wisdom" (*TR* 30.54). For the rational soul proves itself unstable "when it is found to be now skillful, now wanting in skill," whereas it becomes more reliable the more it "participates" in the wisdom and discipline that give the soul form (here, participation means formation and illumination). Rather than the source of its own light, then, the soul is only able to discharge its powers to the extent that it surrenders to the authority of Truth.

> And so the soul, being well aware that it does not judge the looks and motions of bodies by the standard of itself, must at the same time acknowledge that, just as its own nature excels the nature it makes judgments on, so too is it excelled itself by the nature according to which it makes such judgments and on which it is in no way competent to make judgments itself. (*TR* 31.57)

On the other hand, by adhering to the Truth "with total charity" the soul does become in a sense more like God. In fact, it becomes "the very law by which [God] judges all things and on which nobody can pass judgment" (*TR* 31.58). This law Augustine refers to, the "eternal law" of God (Chapter 5, section "Reclaiming the agent"), is a law he will elsewhere associate with discipline (*OO* II.7.25–8.25; Gerber 2012: 96, 97). It is the law that brings humanity in alignment with the truth, the way things are, fulfilling its nature in conformity to Christ. "Some of these [creatures] are *through* this form in such a way as also to be *to* it, such as all rational and intelligent creatures, among which man is so rightly said to have been made to the image and likeness of God" (*TR* 44.82; translator's emphasis).

Having set out these claims about the limits of reason, Augustine turns to make his appeal to his Manichean readers. Thinking of Romanianus he speaks in direct language, asking whether or not they have followed what he wrote. How can they fail to see the truth of these claims, especially that reason depends on truth not vice versa? He imagines their retort, "'Well, you then, you show us what is true' [*ostende quid verum sit*]." If intended as mockery this question is useless; but if voiced in a spirit of reverent inquiry this question is precisely what the Manichees should ask. Suspicious of their motive Augustine offers this response: "If the only answer I gave them was that they should seek that light by which it was clear and certain to them that it is one thing to believe, another to understand, they too would swear that this light could not be seen with the eyes or thought of as being some vast space, and that there is nowhere that it is not at hand to those who are seeking it, and that nothing more sure or serene can be found" (*TR*. 49.96). Only those who ask, seek, and knock find truth, for they alone offer up the prayer of goodwill.

Reaching the summit of his argument in *True Religion*, Augustine traces this journey to its ultimate conclusion: confession of truth. He begins by summing up the steps in the process. First, we are to question our relation to the body: "Ask bodily pleasure what there is to it; you will find it is nothing else but concord ..." Having retrieved this hint from the body below, we are admonished to turn inward to question the soul. "Do not go outside, come back into yourself. It is in the inner self [*interiore homine*] that Truth dwells. And if you find your own nature to be subject to change, transcend even yourself." Of course, we do find our nature subject to change, and so we seek to transcend it toward unchangeable Truth.

So then, direct your course to what the light of reason itself gets its light from. Where, after all, does every good reasoner arrive but at the truth. Since Truth herself, of course, does not reach herself by a process but is herself what reasoners are aiming at, see there the concord which cannot be surpassed, and put yourself in accord with her.

How does one become in accord with the Truth? "*Confess that you are not what she is*" Augustine declares; this is the moment of our reckoning with the truth. For, having sought her "by the desire of your mind," the inner self gathers the weight of its desire for the Truth, "not a carnal pleasure of the lowest sort but a spiritual pleasure of the highest" (*TR* 39.72; emphasis added). Having now re-entered Adam's abandoned place, the inner self experiences a relational transformation.

* * * *

When the rational soul descends from its ascent to the Truth, it inhabits a deep longing and a radically altered perspective. "[I]t gropes, is set afire, gasps with love, is struck by the light of the truth, and turns back, not by choice but out of fatigue, to its own familiar darkness" (*TCWL* I.7.11). "O great God, What kind of eyes shall those be! How pure! How beautiful! How powerful! ... What should we believe? What should we say? Everyday expressions present themselves, but they have been rendered sordid by things of least worth" (*OO* II.19.51). Having traversed across creation, the disciplines, itself, the soul finds freedom from the cares of this world; or at least is on the way to total freedom from the world. "Thus the inner self is being reborn and the outer self is being broken down day to day" (*TR* 40.74). The love of God awakened and incited within it, the soul reconfigures its relation to the other, that is, the neighbor. It is commanded not only to love God but also neighbor, and this requires attending to our immediate situation: the place of the moral self. The location of the neighbor in Augustine's early works adds another valuable perspective on the place of the moral self. Indeed, it confronts us in the sharpest possible way with the challenge raised earlier to his view of creation: Does Augustine truly value the neighbor *qua* neighbor? Or does he simply view the neighbor as a staging point to God?

In Chapter 1, we argued that the genesis of self-awareness is not an act of self-constitution, but an encounter with the other.

Where this encounter has taken place in our reading it has tended to focus on God as *the* Other, giving love of God total dominion over morality, and thus possibly sidelining the command to love the neighbor (O'Donovan 1980: 37). Indeed, insofar as this is the case it negatively impacts Augustine's advice on neighborly love. Let us give examples. First, we are to disdain all ties to family and kin, for love is only true when directed to the eternal; temporal familial attachments only pose a distraction (*TR* 46.88, 89; cf. *R* 1.13.8). Correspondingly, in this life we are to "use" [*uti*] temporal things and defer all "enjoyment" [*fruitio*] to the future vision of God. Finally, although recognizing the needs of body and soul, Augustine argues that "[b]odies ... are not what we are," and that human nature "is to be loved without any reference to the flesh ..." (*TR* 46.89). This view of body finds ample reflection in his praise of ascetic communities in *The Catholic Way of Life* (*TCWL* I.31.65ff). It also reinforces misgivings about his Christology, not to mention his views about the church and the sacraments.

On this evidence, it is tempting to reach the conclusion that Augustine's moral self lacks a place in creation. Through practices engineered for waking the soul and inciting it to stand more upright in reason, Augustine appears to have elevated the soul *above* the world (or outside of it), thus placing a great distance between the self and the other. A possible implication of this outcome for our reading is that it calls into question the first command to love God. Strange as it may seem, the supposed basis of morality may prove to be the feature that subverts moral living. The possibility of a deficient Christology in Augustine only amplifies the challenge to recovering the moral self. Rather than confirm the integrity of creation (i.e., material creation) Augustine's Christ serves to model how to flee the creation—or so it sometimes seems. In fact, the picture is more complicated than this, and one of the complications turns on the act of confession.

The evidence that Augustine took neighbor-love seriously is written all over his early dialogues, letters, and treatises. His conviction that God holds in place the moral self, that God is the "Other" inside being, knowing, willing, does not bring him to disdain that which God has created—at least not in itself—but transforms his encounter with creation *through confession*. Herein lies the breakthrough in his moral conception. In his attempt to guide humanity to its place before God, Augustine opens a space for confessional self-awareness. The nature of confession is that of an ongoing process, a journey on which we call upon the truth to appear. The "we" in this process is an important component; Augustine does not journey on his own in confession. Yes, God is present as its source and destination, but so are many others who will share in his quest. What matters in the first place is the confessional *posture*: for he who confesses does not know all he is saying (or if he is saying anything). Nevertheless, certain truths are axiomatic to confession. They are truths Augustine continues to return to and develop. First, there is the command of Christ to ask, seek, knock. This is absolutely central to a Christian moral life, for it opens the possibility of an encounter with the other. Then, there is the promise of Christ to receive, find, enter. This grounds the hope on which Augustine practices philosophy, emboldening him to call upon his God for assistance ("who can show us the truth?"). Correspondingly, there is the example of the humility of Christ, a virtue increasingly important to Augustine's moral thought (Fitzgerald 2014). In the early works, this virtue takes the form of care for souls as in treating Romanianus and his former co-religionists. It also takes the form of forming Christians in the faith, practicing true charity on behalf of "the little ones" [*parvuli*]. In his account of true charity as building up in love (1 Cor. 1:8) Augustine commits the mature Christian, more advanced on the journey, to sharing the *same* wisdom and *same* sacraments with others. "[A]ny spiritual man who is a good minister of Christ and imitates him to the best of his ability feeds spiritually together with the people on the nourishment provided by the holy scriptures and the divine law ... all have the same food" (*GRM* I.23.40).

> [These Christians] are not concerned, after all, for vain honors and empty praise for themselves but for the profit of those in whose company they have been found worthy to share this life. This, you see, is the law of divine providence, that none should be helped by those above them to the knowledge and reception of God's grace, who have not given the same assistance out of the purest affection to those below them. (*TR* 28.51)

Finally, on the matter of the inside-outside distinction, there is implicit understanding that in turning "in" to the self, one has started to reclaim the abandoned place of moral conscience. "Thus

[God] guides the just person's conscience in his own presence, guides it in the place where no human being sees: he alone sees who discerns what each person thinks and what causes each person delight" (*EP* 7.9). Conscientious knowledge of the self before God opens the self's interior placement to the world it inhabits. In this place one is not sealed off from the world, but better positioned to acknowledge its order and significance. Indeed, one is able to delight in the knowledge that all of creation takes place within God; all of creation confesses God's goodness; and all of creation finds its home in eternity, praising and communing with the angels on high. As Augustine concludes his sweeping *True Religion*,

> So there you are: I worship One God, the One Source of all things, and the Wisdom by which is made wise any soul that is wise, and the very Gift by which is blessed any soul that is blessed. Whichever of the angels abides in him and is able to hear human prayers hears mine in him. Whichever of them holds him as his own good comes to my help in him and does not envy me my sharing in him. (*TR* 55.112)

5

Entering the Problem of Adam's Place

"Free Choice of the Will"

In this chapter, we approach our final pathway in this study by focusing on the early dialogue *Free Choice of the Will* (AD 388–395). Centered on the act of responsible moral judgment, *Free Choice of the Will*—though a poor translation, as we shall see—also serves as a spiritual exercise in shaping moral awareness. That is, it is much less an argument *about* the will and more an invitation to *reclaim* human agency ("willing"). In this, it provides another path to the moral self.

As noted in the last chapter, Augustine's context in this period is his ongoing battle with the stubborn Manichees. That battle turns substantially on the phrase "if willing" [*si volet*], a condition voiced regularly in earlier works (cf. *TR* 35.65). If only the Manichees would desire the truth, and if only they were seekers who desired to find it (Mt. 7:7). As an exercise examining that condition of willing, *Free Choice of the Will* fits a clear moral trajectory. It amplifies a question already there from the start, yet deliberately set aside for its own special treatment.

At the same time, this dialogue is as controversial today as when Augustine first defended it at length. A diverse set of interests seem invariably to crowd around it, and while some heap praise (philosophers) and others level critiques (historians and theologians), none seriously questions its immediate and long-term impact. Those who admire it might register the dialogue as Augustine's debut as "first philosopher of the will" (Arendt 1971: 84ff). That is to say, its distinctive contribution to history is to paint the first portrait of the self-determining moral agent (Dihle 1982; Kahn 1988; for the debate in general, see Irwin 1992). For critics, on the other hand, it also bears witness to Augustine's native venture in a "humanist" direction. Not only does it exhibit a lack of theological depth, at least according to standards set later by Augustine, but it sometimes comes across as "more Pelagian than Pelagius" (Brown 2000 [1967]: 141)—a bold claim indeed. Moreover, it is claimed that the dialogue shows evidence that Augustine changed his mind about the nature of the will (Wetzel 1992; Lettieri 2001). The length of time it took him to finish it suggests this, as does his long entry defending it in *Revisions* (for an overview, Madec 1996). In fact, the charge of a change in opinion casts a shadow over Augustine's early corpus and development. It suggests that the path we have traveled so far, the path to the moral self, is one that Augustine did not want us to take. Is that true?

For this chapter, stopping well short of resolving these debates, we propose that to grasp the animating purpose of this work requires drawing on the storyline we discussed in Genesis 3. Building on the work of Simon Harrison among others (S. Harrison 2006; C. Harrison 2006; Stock 2010; Topping 2012), we argue that this dialogue has a central moral purpose that grows out of Augustine's earlier studies in self-knowledge: to lead us to a place in which we reclaim the will—the place of the moral self—and there begin to confess the agent's origin, nature, and condition. In this way, the dialogue offers one more attempt to re-enter Adam's place for the sake of the truth. As we shall see, it involves not only avoiding Adam's error—blaming God for evil—but also accepting the invitation to acknowledge humanity's position, "Where are you?" (Gn. 3:9). To what extent Augustine's answer to this question proves adequate— to what extent, that is, it is faithfully "Augustinianism"—becomes a less important issue than identifying his strategy for awakening the soul to its partaking in Adam's story.

Starting from faith

Not ignoring the philosophical questions this dialogue provokes, this chapter nevertheless argues that *Free Choice of the Will* does not offer a comprehensive theory of human moral action. Rather, in keeping with Augustine's theological concerns, its purpose is to manifest God's goodness and justice (i.e., to confess them) by locating human beings *in* their moral condition. The intended outcome of this process of confession by location is a fuller recognition of our place in God's world, and a fuller understanding of the faith we already possess (Is. 7:9; FCW I.2.4); for faith plays a crucial role in shaping this work, providing its basic starting point (*initium*) from the very first lines. More precisely, it is faith that gives rise to the "problem of evil"—or at least one variant of it—and faith that supports the reader's efforts to address it. To clarify the role of faith, this section begins by engaging an important passage in *Confessions* book VII.

* * * *

Before his famous encounter with the "books of the Platonists," Augustine struggled to come to terms with how to think about evil. More specifically, he struggled over the question of evil's origin: a question first put to him by his former co-religionists, the Manichees, who raised it and other questions to disturb the Catholic faithful (Lieu 1985: 119). Recalling this experience in *Confessions* book III, he impugns the Manichees for their materialist outlook:

> I was being subtly maneuvered [at the time] into accepting the views of those stupid deceivers by the question they constantly asked me about the origin of evil, and whether God was confined to a material form with hair and nails, and whether people who practiced polygamy, killed human beings and offered animal sacrifices could be considered righteous. Being ignorant of these matters I was very disturbed by the questions, and supposed that I was approaching the truth when I was in fact moving away from it. I did not know that evil is nothing but the diminishment of good to the point where nothing at all is left. How could I see that, I whose power of sight was restricted to seeing material shapes with my eyes and imaginary forms with my mind? (C III.7.12)

We have already dealt with how the Manichees read Scripture, or rather how they fail and refuse to read Scripture (Chapter 4, section "Turning inside out"), and closely tied to that refusal is their invoking the origin of evil, acting as if the question *by itself* proved a point. In fact, all it proved, as Augustine later realized, is that the Manichees could not elevate their reason above the body (Lee 1999: 11). It showed up their inability to stay true to God, betraying their self-abasement to the material form of creation.

That is not all it betrayed, however. In addition to ignorance in metaphysical truths the question revealed the depths of Manichean self-deception. Not knowing who they were or where they were in the world, the Manichees pretended not to be there at all. They did this not simply by declaring their souls divine, as Chapter 4 explored, but also by denying their complicity in evil. Of course, that was partly what made them attractive. It is certainly one of the things which attracted Augustine, for it offered a tidy solution to a thorny moral problem: not simply the problem of whence evil derives (*unde malum*) but more personally the problem of *our own* evil-making (*unde malum faciamus*; *FCW* I.2.4). Metaphysically, by denying the primacy of good the Manichees treated evil's origin as insoluble (Evans 1990: 13). Evil always has been a part of reality, making the question of its origin a matter of clarification, enlightenment. Morally, this removed any need to confront evil as it no longer presented a personal *problem* to the agent (Lee 1999: xii). If evil always has been and will be with us, if evil is woven into the fabric of the "universe" (Chapter 4, section "Turning outside in"), to ask about its origin or "cause" in humans is like asking why stones fall to the ground when dropped (*FCW* III.1.2). In short, by ontologizing the nature of evil the Manichees kept evil from terrorizing their conscience.

For Augustine, this opportunity for absolving the conscience proved an offer too attractive to ignore upfront. As G.R. Evans observes,

> The Manichean explanation took away the need to search his heart and to avert his eyes from the troubled state of his own conscience, and allowed him to turn his attention to the world, to argue grand issues concerning the structure of the universe. It allowed him to make compartments in his thinking, and to shut off from his gaze those things within him which were to trouble him all his life when once he began to think about them clearly. (Evans 1990: 15)

Such compartmentalized thinking would continue with Augustine until his encounter with Ambrose and the books of the Platonists.

In *Confessions* book VII, after listening to Ambrose preach, he becomes convinced that God's nature is "imperishable, inviolable and unchangeable" (C VII.1.1), shaking him free from his Manichean materialism. However, he is still struggling with the problem of evil, and is realizing the dangers that surround his inquiry. "[W]hatever it might be," he recalls thinking, "I saw that ... I must beware of looking for it in such a way as to be forced into believing that the immutable God was changeable, lest I become myself the very thing I was trying to trace." For, through "their inquiry into the origin of evil" the Manichees "had waxed full of malice, more ready to claim that your substance was vulnerable to evil than that their own perpetrated it" (C VII.3.4). But despite this good insight the pressure kept mounting. Where did evil come from, if God is all good? Where did it find a foothold, if God created all good things? Another error appeared to be lurking in his way of framing the question. "So I was seeking the origin of evil, but seeking in an evil way, and failing to see the evil inherent in my search itself" (C VII.5.7). Part of that "evil inherent in my search" was his metaphysical failure to know the nature of evil (or to un-know it). But part of it as well, as this Chapter explores, was his *moral* failure to claim responsibility *for* evil: to occupy the place of Adam.

* * * *

Despite struggling to comprehend the origin of evil, Augustine states that he continued in his fledgling Christian faith.

> Faith in your Christ, our Lord and Savior, as I found it in the Catholic Church, still persisted steadfastly in my heart, though it was a faith still in many ways unformed, wavering and at variance with the norm of her teaching. Yet my mind did not abandon it, but drank it in ever more deeply as the days passed. (C VII.5.7)

Keep that in mind as we proceed with our reading. Now, turning to *Free Choice of the Will* book I, we explore how Augustine frames the problem of evil by guiding his reader to identify the question.

That reader, the student Evodius (or anonymous; S. Harrison 2006: 32–33), steps up to the plate, setting off the discussion with a pressing theological issue: "Please tell me whether God is not the author of evil." The upfront question quickly captures our attention.

It is as if we have been dropped into an ongoing conversation with no introduction or dedicatory address to prepare us. Plunged into the middle, *in medias res*, we are transported back to the beginning of all things, creation itself. Evodius is enquiring into the origin of evil. As we know, that question could spiral in dubious directions, revealing an "evil inherent in our search." Perhaps on this account Augustine requests clarification, wanting to know the kind of evil he has in mind. There are, he says, at least two types: (a) the evil one commits on one's own; and (b) the evil one suffers as punishment (*FCW* I.1.1). Naturally both, says Evodius, yet Augustine is not done. Instead, he calls to mind what the two already believe: their shared framework of faith that will guide their discussion.

> Well, if you know or believe that God is good (it is blasphemous to think otherwise), then He does not *do* evil. On the other hand, if we grant that God is just (denying it is irreligious), then He rewards the good; by the same token, He hands out punishments to evildoers, punishments that are doubtless evils to those who suffer them. Accordingly, if no one pays the penalties unjustly—which we must believe since we believe that the world is governed by divine providence—then God is indeed the author of evils of type (b), though not in any way the author of evils of type (a). (*FCW* I.1.1)

God is good, so God does not commit evil. God is just, so God is right to punish evil. No other conclusions are permitted by our faith; and yet, we wonder, why should faith stand in the way of philosophy? Why should we presuppose these things about God? The reason becomes clear as the conversation proceeds. Faith does not inhibit the inquiry, but sharpens it.

Spinning his wheels Evodius offers a second question: "Then is there *some other author* of the evil we have found not to come from God?" (*FCW* I.1.1; emphasis added). In other words, if God is not the author of evil, perhaps some other being or Being is responsible. An improvement on the first but still not the right one. The question tempts the answer one receives from Manichaeism: evil is the result of a single Being rivaling God. Wanting desperately to avoid this dualistic trap, Augustine continues to push Evodius to consider other options. Yes, he affirms, evil does have "some other author," but really many authors who commit evil acts. We must not trace evil to a single rival entity, but rather hold individual agents responsible for it "through the will [*voluntate*]." For the first time, Augustine signals a way through the question. It is only through the will that evil is committed, which means our focus ought to turn to the will as complicit. Unfortunately, this way is still hidden to Evodius. He is still hung up on a single author of evil, now peering *behind* individual authors for the source. "Perhaps no one sins unless he has learned how. But if that is true, I ask: *From whom did we learn how to sin?*" (*FCW* I.1.2; emphasis added). Again, an improvement from the first and the second, for at least it has Evodius noting evil's interpersonal dimension. His problem is in thinking that evil can be *learned*, which Augustine points out is technically impossible: neither learning nor teaching can take evil as an object (following a Platonic insight). If no one learns evil, and no one teaches evil, the conclusion to be reached is *no other entity* authorizes evil. Augustine states plainly, "stop trying to track down some mysterious teacher! If he is evil he is not a teacher; and if he is a teacher he is not evil" (*FCW* I.2.4).

If no one *else* authorizes evil, where does that leave us? Evodius by this point is no doubt exasperated, but will offer up a final fourth attempt at a question. "Very well. Now that you have pushed me into admitting that we do not *learn* to do evil, tell me: How is it that we *do* evil [*unde malum faciamus*]?" (*FCW* I.2.4; translator's emphasis). Here, Evodius is knocking on the door to the truth. He has shifted attention from a hidden author of evil to the notion that evil has its origin in us (*we* do evil). In this way, he has cast a spotlight on the self, representing the human as a *responsible moral agent*. We can now, it seems, begin a search for the origin, as Augustine makes clear by his positive response.

> You are raising a question that hounded me while I was young; when I was worn out it caused my downfall, landing me in the company of heretics [Manichees]. I was so injured by this fall, and so buried under such vast heaps of empty tales, that had the love of finding the truth not succeeded in requesting and receiving divine succor for me, I would not have been able to dig my way out and breathe again, recovering my earlier freedom of enquiry. And since such pains were taken in my case to set me free from that question, I shall guide you on the same route that I used to escape. God will be at hand and make us understand what we

have come to believe. Indeed, we are well aware that this is to take the course prescribed by the prophet, who says: "Unless you believe you shall not understand" [Is. 7:9]. (*FCW* I.2.4)

A few aspects of this passage command our attention. We learn that Evodius' fourth question to Augustine, *unde malum faciamus?*, had plagued a younger Augustine for an indeterminate period. In fact, he says it prompted his turn to Manichaeism, inducing his acceptance of "empty tales" about evil. He adds that this undercut his "earlier freedom of enquiry" which later he recovered by his "love of finding out the truth" [*amor inveniendi veri*]. Oddly, this account does not match his story in *Confessions*. This question never appears in book III or *The Happy Life*, both of which link Augustine's downfall to *Hortensius* (and his pride; Chapter 3, Section "Seeking and doubting"). His intention in this case may not be to tell history, though, but to model for us a method of how to narrate the self. By introducing in this moment the "first-personal perspective," he is amplifying the "conditions" for examining human agency (Harrison 1999). As Brian Stock has shown, one of Augustine's great achievements was to integrate personal narrative into knowledge of the self (or vice versa; Stock 2010: 181–228). Personal stories, although insufficient *grounds* for ethical judgment (as in Plato; Stock 2010: 59; Rist 2014), can support ethical *insight* into the nature of the agent (*pace* Plato; Stock 2010: 59). In view of Evodius' fourth question *unde malum faciamus?*, such a method has the effect of instantiating self-awareness that *I*, not an alien race of darkness or second soul (*TTS*), am an agent who is responsible for committing evil acts.

Finally, we draw attention to his invocation of faith as the ground and starting point for examining the origin of evil. After citing Isaiah, Augustine lists off several beliefs which he claims are essential for the dialogue to proceed. "Take heart! Believe as you do: there is no better belief, even if the reason why it is so is hidden. Holding God in the highest esteem is surely the most authentic beginning of religiousness [*exordium pietatis*]" (*FCW* I.25). Those beliefs include claims about God's goodness and justice, that God created all things, that God is omnipotent and unchangeable; in short, all beliefs tied to the doctrine of creation. Moreover, as we observed from *Confessions* book VII, they are beliefs that shield the soul from the fatal human temptation: to blame God for evil. Thus, having secured the essential ground for understanding, Augustine embarks on the process of reclaiming Adam's place: that is, the place of conscience.

* * * *

Book I is often framed as a failed experiment. As a project gone wrong only to be abandoned in book II. A mess in many directions, it never seems to settle on a single line of enquiry or a focused debate. And that is setting aside its more shocking suggestions on the matter of human autonomy and the soul's pre-existence. That may not be the whole story, however, and may even sell short the goal of the book. According to Harrison, book I is a beginning (*exordium*) that opens more questions than it proposes to answer. So much is indicated in Augustine's conclusion when he invokes a familiar verse to set up book II:

> I would like you to believe that in this discussion we have, so to speak, been knocking at the door [Mt. 7:7] of profound and abstruse matters that need to be explored. Once we begin to enter into their inner recesses, with God's help, you surely will judge *how much distance* there is between this discussion and those to follow, and *how much the latter* surpass the former, not only in the sagacity of the investigation but also in the grandeur of the issues and the most resplendent light of the truth. May there be enough religiousness in us that divine providence allows us to hold to and complete the course we have plotted. (*FCW* I.16.35)

For Harrison, book I takes off at "beginner's level." It is grounded in "everyday examples (murder and adultery) and simple concepts (law and order)." Book II takes off at the "intermediate" level. It deals with headier topics like wisdom and number (S. Harrison 2006: 31). Book III, the final step, reaches the summit by raising difficult topics in "advanced" philosophy (i.e., theology; S. Harrison 2006: 13; Rist 2014: 353). None of this is arranged accidentally, Harrison insists, and Augustine is not "experimenting" at random with his subject (*pace* O'Connell 1970). His purpose is to show us a "way into the will;" to model how to re-claim and inhabit moral agency. From the personalized narrative that opens book I, to the overarching narrative that emerges in book III, he wants to establish above all our place in this world, revealing both good and bad aspects of our place (i.e., good and evil). For Harrison this begins right away in book I with Augustine's opening analysis of moral and legal scenarios (Bruner 2000: 37–62; cited by Stock 2010: 149).

Taking up the subject of law and morality, Augustine begins to trace the lineaments of his view of moral conscience (though without mentioning conscience; Svensson 2013). After establishing Evodius' question of whence *we* do evil, he raises the question of what it is to *do* evil. This is a move for which Augustine is famous (Lee 1999: 11). Replacing *unde malum?* with the question *quid malum?* forces the Manichees to define the nature of evil, exposing the crudity of their materialist outlook. After all, as he puts it in *The Manichean Way of Life*, such a question helps thinkers avoid the greatest absurdity of all: seeking "the origin of something of which we are ignorant" (*TMWL* II.2.2). Thus as he did already in *True Religion* he begins turning outward to evaluate the claims of authority. He asks Evodius to consider what makes an act evil. Why do we condemn things like adultery and murder?

Taking his cue from the Sermon on the Mount, Augustine guides the conversation to the following conclusion: murder and adultery are definitely evil, and they are evil on the authority of "eternal law" not the "temporal law" (*FCW* I.6.14–15). This authoritative eternal law, also referred to as "supreme reason," is said to be impressed upon the human moral subject: "stamped on us [*impressa nobis*]: It is the law according to which it is just for all things to be completely in order [*ordinatissima*]" (*FCW* I.6.15). Echoing language for the image of God (*EP* 4.8.; Chapter 4, section "Turning outside in"), he suggests that by obeying and enacting this law the soul begins to be conformed to the image and likeness of God. This is happening right now with the likes of Evodius. He is learning how to stand on his own two feet, rather than surrender his free judgment to temporal authority (*FCW* I.4.10). He is becoming the very law by which the Truth judges reality (cf. *TR* 31.58; 4.3), thus reflecting God's truth into the world through intelligence.

In addition, Augustine's appeal to the idea of "free judgment" [*liberum arbitrium*] sets the stage for future accounts of the work of moral conscience. Although the term *conscientia* does not appear in book I (it appears twice in book III, *pace* Svensson 2013), its presence is intimated in the act of free judgment that illumines the hidden evil in adultery and murder. This evil, he says, originates in "lust" [*libido*] or "desire" [*cupiditas*] (*FCW* I.3.8–4.9), which functions as the inner spring of outer evil acts (cf. Sermon on the Mount). Through exercising the act of free judgment in conscience—free because able to stand in judgment over desire ("conscience as evaluation of our moral disposition itself;" Svensson 2013: 46)—Evodius gains greater command over the nature of evil action. "I have regained my wits now. I am glad to know so plainly the nature of that blameworthy desire referred to as 'lust'" (*FCW* I.5.11). In fact, he is beginning to come to terms with the fact that humans commit evil to achieve a *good* end, freedom from fear. However, they often fail to pursue this correctly by seeking freedom from fear from objects they can lose (*FCW* I.4.10–5.11). In so doing, even though no temporal law will condemn them, they are accountable in conscience to a "more powerful and hidden law" (*FCW* I.5.12). Thus, as he marches to the place of moral conscience Augustine applauds his discovery of a higher moral truth. "I approve and endorse this distinction of yours [between temporal and eternal law]. Even though it is just a beginning and not complete, it confidently aims at exalted heights" (*FCW* I.5.13).

Reclaiming the agent

Early in his discussion of the temporal law, Augustine admonishes Evodius not to give up on his search. "Have courage, and set out along the roads of reason with the support of religiousness. There is nothing so demanding or difficult that is not made completely plain and easy with God's assistance" (*FCW* I.6.14). The statement, which reaffirms Augustine's commitment to faith, also exhibits a peculiar confidence in the powers of reason. This has raised some doubts among readers of this period as to whether Augustine grasps the true depth of the problem of evil. Given how much he once struggled with the problem, it is reasonable to suspect that something else is afoot, and that his early positive statements have an important role to play.

As noted earlier, Harrison proposes that the aim of book I is to place us on the way to recovering the will. After inviting us to investigate the origin of evil, the book grounds its inquiry in a

Christian moral ontology that draws for its basis on the doctrine of creation (*exordium pietatis*). Then, having located the right question and perspective, the book begins to lay a claim on the self *qua* agent. It begins to locate Evodius in the place of "the will" [*voluntas*] as an initial response to the problem of evil. If so, and before mapping the path he takes to get there, we must first address the question: what does Augustine mean by *voluntas*?

By *voluntas*, Augustine means a basic activity of the soul; *voluntas* is something one is doing all the time. It is a condition of human nature much as being and knowing, and for that reason must be treated in conjunction with those terms. By translating *voluntas* as "the will," however, one tempts an identification with the modern moral subject. This notion of a self-made and self-willed self posits a will operating outside the constraints of human nature, a will totally "free" of one's nature altogether, as if the will had no object but the object will chooses. By conjuring up an image of a faculty or power in orbit around the soul's lower activities and pursuits, "the will" projects not only a fanciful view of the self, it also distracts attention from the problem at hand: namely, the self's implication in perpetuating evil. Consequently, many scholars work to challenge this conception by translating *voluntas* through circumlocution: for example, "act of willing" (Burnell 2005: 55), "loving will" (Rist 2014: 80–82), even the moral self (i.e., *voluntas* as the occurrent-dispositional moral self; Rist 2014: 31; citing Byers 2006). Their motive in each case is to avoid reification by allowing *voluntas* to name "how we are" in the world; or in terms of this study, "where we are" and "where we are going;" for will is closely tied to the movement of love.

* * * *

In book I, the approach Augustine takes to "the will"—we shall retain this translation for ease of reference—starts off by returning to the question of order. "How a human being may be completely in order within himself." In keeping with his "beginner's level" method in book I, he draws Evodius to attend to the most obvious facts: in this case, the fact that he is alive and desires life; a maneuver labeled by some "the Augustinian cogito" (S. Harrison 2006: 80). "Tell me" Augustine requests, "whether you are completely certain that you are alive" (*FCW* I.7.16). Here, the cogito aims to furnish a place: to provide a firm foothold for Evodius' inquiry. By drawing Evodius' attention to the fact that he is alive Augustine appeals to a fact *prior to* Evodius' reflection: a "pre-reflexive" (Turner 1995: 85ff) knowing of his own self-existence, conveyed into being by an innate desire for life.

As a philosophical and psychological strategy in debate, Augustine's cogito brings to light a lover's prior disposition. It awakens a lover's to knowledge of the love for life itself: an inclination which finds its fulfillment in eternal life. As Augustine declares in *Free Choice of the Will* book III, "The more you love to be, the more you will desire eternal life" (*FCW* III.7.21; cf. *S* II.1.1) And in *True Religion*, deploying a similar cogitarian strategy: "Eternal life, after all, surpasses temporal life by its intensity of life ..." (*TR* 49.97). In *The Happy Life*, Augustine opens by asking his students to answer whether they know that they are alive (*THL* 2.7). That they know and affirm this is essential and good, but only sets the stage for their quest for the happy life—the point of the book. Here, the cogito is not a proposition or "proof," but a placeholder disclosing the true object of delight: life immortal. In that sense we could call it a locating device that is used to beckon lovers to confess their position, establishing "I am alive" as a starting point to knowledge. Thus, through integrating this acknowledgment of living into knowledge of their quest for some end called the happy life—or the completely ordered life—lovers gain awareness of their being on the way, which sets them up to discover their moral status as an agent.

All this comes to the fore later in book I. At present, Augustine's purpose is to establish right order: the order that prevails not after sin has been committed, "postlapsarian," but the order that prevails in the original plan of creation, the beginning of Adam and Eve. This is evident by the idealism informing his account. Having established Evodius' knowledge of himself as alive, he then moves to make a distinction between "*being alive*" and "*knowing yourself to be alive*" (*FCW* I.7.16). The distinction holds the key to becoming completely ordered. We do not merely exist as rocks or as trees, nor merely do we live as plants or animals do (Chapter 4, section "Turning outside in"). Instead, we humans have the gift of "understanding" [*intellegere*], which places us above mere "being" [*esse*] and "living" [*vivere*]. From this, Augustine concludes that to establish true order, humans must assign a dominant role to the power of reason. "That by which humans are ranked above animals ... if it dominates and commands the rest of what a human consists in, then that human being is completely in order" (*FCW* I.8.18). And from here, Augustine exults in the superiority of reason—now called mind—by observing how virtually nothing can throw the mind off its game. Not even God, who exceeds us by nature, can overthrow the mind given his own good nature.

But this raises a question: why is mind overthrown? Why is it that humans behave in disordered and irrational ways? The only answer is humanity deposes itself. Human beings, no one else, are the responsible agents. "Nothing makes the mind a devotee of desire but its own will and free choice [*propria voluntas et liberum arbitrium*]" (*FCW* I.11.21). This conclusion re-connects us with the opening lines. There, Augustine resisted any attempt to shift the blame. He resisted any attempt at an appeal to another author, especially God, to bear responsibility for the evil of humanity. Now, with his new theory on how this came about—the mind's *propria voluntas et liberum arbitrium*—he proposes a new vision of postlapsarian human life. For those rejecting wisdom as well as those attempting to regain it (*pace* Wetzel 1992: 87, n3; citing Babcock 1988: 38–39), the journey we call life is sadly replete with moral struggle. Augustine knows this from personal experience; thus, he pauses to map the stages in his (postlapsarian) journey.

> Lust dominates the mind and drags it back and forth, despoiled of the richness of virtue, poor and needy; at one moment taking falsehoods for truths and even making a practice of defending them [his rhetoric training], at another rejecting what it had previously accepted [his childhood religion] and nonetheless rushing to other falsehoods [his Manichean years]; now withholding its assent and often in dread of clear lines of argument [his dallying with the Skeptics]; now despairing of the whole enterprise of finding the truth, lingering deep within the shadows of foolishness [the effects of skepticism]; now struggling towards the light of understanding but again falling back from it due to exhaustion [his reading of the Platonists, revealing the depth of his fallen condition]. (*FCW* I.11.22)

Just as he did in the early parts of book I, Augustine inserts his own story into the problem of evil. Exhibiting the "penalties" he suffered along the way, he throws out the idealism of his prelapsarian vision, and begins to open a new trajectory to the place of "the will." We turn there now.

* * * *

After gesturing to the question of the origin of soul (revisited in book III), Augustine abruptly changes course to address another question. "So tell me: We have a will, do we not?" (*FCW* I.12.25). In fact, the question is more indirect than that. The Latin reads, *sitne aliqua nobis voluntas:* "There is something we call our will, isn't there?" King's translation can tempt us to objectify the will, whereas Augustine seems to be gesturing to the phenomenon of willing. His is asking, do we recognize this willing in motion, do we understand ourselves as taking part in its occurrence? Though regarded by many as a trivial question, this moment marks for Harrison the decisive point in the book. The whole dialogue hinges on how readers respond; more precisely, on whether or not they are *willing* to respond. Harrison comments: "We have here what Augustine might call the beginnings, the starting point, the 'inchoatio,' of even the 'exordium' of a considered concept of the will. Voluntas has been through some sort of process here" (S. Harrison 2006: 71).

It has, and this process traces back to the beginning, back to the initial declaration of faith. Having confirmed his pious belief in God the Creator, Evodius demonstrated by his willingness to adjust his approach, and by putting up with Augustine's interjections along the way, that he desires nothing more than to seek and find the truth; that he desires nothing more than to understand what he believes (*intellectus fidei*). Even so, Evodius stumbles in replying to Augustine. Declaring "I don't know" [*nescio*] to Augustine's simple question, he threatens to derail their forward momentum in the dialogue. Prepared for this response, Augustine quickly steps in: "Do you not *want* to know this?" (*FCW* I.12.25; emphasis added), he asks a wavering Evodius. In taking this step back to question his motive, he again courts Evodius' innate desire for the truth. If Evodius re-confirms his desire for the truth, he not only authenticates his status as a philosopher (the initial goal at Cassiciacum), but also now "proves" the very truth of which he is ignorant: the reality of the will. Hence, by confessing his desire to know truth, he instantiates that truth through his will to participate. "That we have a will [*habere nos voluntatem*] cannot be denied, I admit. Go on; let us see what you are going to do with this" (*FCW* I.12.25). The import of this moment is still lost on Evodius, and yet he resolves to continue on the way. His statement "we have a will" links to the question "whence do we do evil," but not as an answer to the question *simpliciter* but only as a starting point for further inquiry. Thus, we agree with Harrison's claim that this passage offers a variant on the Augustinian cogito.

> Evodius knows that he has a will, not because it is self-evident knowledge which one cannot fail to have, but because it is self-evident knowledge which one *can* fail to have. Precisely in my ability to know that I have a will, and to fail to want to know that, I can see the self-evidence of my responsibility. (S. Harrison 2006: 113)

> Harrison goes further to describe this event as an ultimatum similar to the one in *The Academics*. Either we step up and take responsibility for our search, or we relax on the mountain of our so-called achievement, forsaking the real happiness that lies up ahead.

> Evodius stands, as it were, at a crossroads, or perhaps we might say on the edge of an abyss. To one side no questions, no answers, no dialogue, no wisdom, no friendship, no happiness; to the other at least the desire for these things … The threat, and indeed the challenge, for Augustine, of scepticism lies in its capacity to induce *desperatio veri*, the despair of finding the truth. (S. Harrison 2006: 113–114)

In that sense we can understand Augustine's retort that he will not proceed without Evodius' assent.

> I am not required to answer your questions unless you are willing to know [*volenti scire*] what you are asking about. Henceforth, unless you want [*velis*] to attain wisdom, I should not discuss these matters with you. Finally, you cannot be my friend unless you want [*velis*] my well-being. Then you, for your part, will see in respect of yourself whether you have no will [*utrum tibi voluntas nulla*] for the happy life. (*FCW* I.12.25)

"Then you ... will see." What will he see? He will see his own will at work toward the happy life, laboring and striving for the one true good. This striving is not unlike the weight of his love: it is taking Evodius somewhere he desires, and if that somewhere is happiness and communion with God (and Augustine), he will hasten to affirm what he already shows: an upright will that desires the good, or in short, a "good will" [*bona voluntas*].

At this point Augustine pauses to discuss the goodwill. He puts forth the idea that Evodius' goodwill is in fact the very *object* of his search for the happy life. We have returned, it seems, to the original prelapsarian creation, a state in which humanity stood upright before God. "Should we then not rejoice a little that in the mind we have something—I am speaking of the good will itself—in comparison with which all the things we have mentioned are completely unimportant, things in pursuit of which we see many people spare no efforts and avoid no dangers?" (*FCW* I.12.25). Indeed, Augustine sounds frankly Kantian in his claim that nothing at all should be desired *but* this will.

> Therefore, anyone who has a good will (whose superiority we have been discussing for a long time now) would embrace this one thing [the good will] as an unsurpassable delight—on the one hand pleasing himself, on the other hand taking complete satisfaction and rejoicing to think of it, judging how great it is and how it cannot be stolen or taken away against his will. (*FCW* I.13.27; cf. Kant's *Groundwork*, 4:393)

This argument's Stoic dimensions have been noted before, and one discerns above all a most glaring and startling absence: where is God? Is it really the case, as Augustine asserts, that "anyone who wills to live rightly and honorably, if he wills himself to will this instead of transient goods, acquires so great a possession with such ease [*tanta facilitate*] that having what he willed is nothing other for him than willing it"? (*FCW* I.13.29).

The term *bona voluntas* is not uncommon in Augustine. In a contemporary work *The Manichean Way of Life*, he locates a goodwill in the context of seeking truth: "For we had to show you the door [Mt. 7:7], over which you despair and over which you cause the ignorant to despair. For nothing brings you inside but a good will [*voluntas bona*] that divine mercy has rendered peaceful ..."

(*TMWL* II.7.10). Elsewhere, the goodwill stands to correct perverse desire, though with God's help (*TCWL* I.34.76; cf. *TR* 12.24), while a bad or "evil will" is the sole source of perversion: "sin exists nowhere but in the will ..." (*TTS* 10.12). But here, having isolated the will from the search, and failing to mention our need for God's assistance ("with such ease"), Augustine appears almost to divinize the goodwill itself (or perhaps "Good Will," following Phillip Cary), thus abandoning his earlier judgment on our postlapsarian condition. The key assumption here, according to Phillip Cary, is Paul's line "Christ the Virtue of God and the Wisdom of God" (1 Cor. 1:24). Cary contends, "Just as at Cassiciacum the immutable Reason and Truth we seek to know is Christ the Wisdom of God, so in book I of *On Free Choice* [*of the Will*] the immutable Good Will we should wish to enjoy is Christ the Virtue of God" (Cary 2000: 111).

Yet, here again, Cary ignores the image of God. For it is precisely by enacting God's law through conscience that the soul begins to order itself *to* the image and likeness. It begins to re-claim its position in Adam, uncovering the goodwill that is part of our condition. After declaring how "easy" it is to will the goodwill (which is the happy life), Augustine again reverts back to our postlapsarian condition. "Then *why do they not all attain* [the happy life]? ... That is, how does someone gain the happy life through the will, when everyone wants to be happy and yet so many are unhappy?" (*FCW* I.14.30). The answer, of course, is that not everyone wills "rightly," which is to say that not everyone loves the eternal law within (*FCW* I.15.31). What else does eternal law command, moreover, but to "turn our love aside from temporal things and to turn it, purified, towards eternal things" (*FCW* I.15.32)? In this way, Augustine sets up the next set of arguments (books II and III) that demonstrates God's goodness as the object of delight, the condition for the possibility of recovering the goodwill.

Approaching understanding

Although our journey stops shy of book II and book III (they were written after AD 391), we want to briefly comment on the conclusions they reach. Let us return first of all to *Confessions* book VII. What was the error in Augustine's search for the origin of evil? Not only his metaphysical error of materialism, resolved upon reading the books of the Platonists. But also his moral error of avoiding God's question, ignoring his implication in the problem of evil. He was asking the right question, *unde malum?*, yet without including himself in the question, *unde malum faciamus?* In book VII, he describes his attempt to solve the former. "I conjured up before my mind's eye the whole of creation"—yet notably not himself as a creature in creation. "I pictured [creation] as enormous ... I imagined you, Lord, who are infinite in every possible respect, surrounding and penetrating it in its every part ... and I reflected, 'Look, this is God, and these are the things God has created ... '" And, since "God is good," God created good things. And yet the question remains: "Where, then, is evil; where did it come from and how did it creep in?" (C VII.5.7). On and on does Augustine continue with this question, yet never once *turning the question on himself as an agent*. It is only after ascending through the books of the Platonists that he grasps the moral condition that prevents his ascent. "I inquired then what villainy might be, but I found no substance, only the perversity of a will twisted away from you, God, the supreme substance, towards the depths—a will that throws away its life within and swells with vanity abroad" (C VII.16.22).

To some extent, this is the lesson of *Free Choice of the Will*. Its goal is not to offer up a causal account of evil—though *voluntas* is obviously involved—but to locate the human agent *in* the problem of evil; a process that began when Evodius acknowledged the will (book I). Then in book II, Augustine develops an argument showing God is the source of goodness and truth, and bestowed on human creatures the gift of free will (an intermediate good) which, however, we "throw away" and abuse. In the end, there is no "answer" to the origin of evil (Brown 1978). "If I were to reply to your question [where does evil will come from] that I do not know, perhaps you will then be the sadder, but I will at least have replied truthfully. What is nothing cannot be known." And, fully aware of the dangers now afoot, he admonishes Evodius not to fall to Adam's error (Chapter 2, section "Locating Adam in Genesis 3"), attempting to trace the origin of evil back to God.

> Hold firm with resolute religiousness that you will not encounter, by sensing or understanding ... any good thing which is not from God .... there is no nature that is not from God. Thus see what the movement of 'turning away' [from God] pertains to. We

admit that this movement is sin, since it is a defective movement, and every defect is from nothing. Be assured that this movement does *not* pertain to God! (*FCW* II.20.54; translator's emphasis)

Instead, his last step is to identify this movement as a "voluntary" movement "placed within our power." "If you fear it," Augustine advises, "you must not will it; if you do not will it, it will not exist." Alas, if only it were as simple as that! Since not, he recalls us to the starting point of faith. "But since we cannot rise of our own accord as we fell of it, let us hold on with firm faith to the right hand of God stretched out to us from above, namely our Lord Jesus Christ; let us await Him with resolute hope and desire Him with burning charity" (*FCW* II.20.54).

Here in book II, Augustine unfolds another layer to the problematic position in which humanity finds itself. He states the problem succinctly in book III: "[Most people] are quicker to excuse their sins than to confess them" (*FCW*. III.2.5). Of course, that pattern was set long ago, at the height of the drama in Genesis 3. In response to God's question Adam and Eve tried to dissemble; on this tactic Augustine comments, "to talk like this is really to accuse rather than excuse oneself" (*TCG* XIV.14). Even so, this is the *modus operandi* of Adam's descendants: a persistent resistance to a reckoning with the truth. In book III, Augustine's goal is to defeat that resistance, delivering genuine seekers to the place of moral conscience. "[If only] from all their bones and the pith of conscience they cried out: 'I said: My Lord, be merciful to me! Heal my soul, for I have sinned against You!' [Ps. 40:5]—well, *then* they would be led by certain paths of divine mercy into wisdom" (*FCW* III.2.5).

But here, the question is: how to become that seeker? And if Augustine for a while could defer on that question, or even assume a simplistic understanding of the will (as many allege), in book III the question starts to niggle more and more, and Augustine begins to struggle toward a proper understanding. His key phrase repeated over and over is "if willing" [*si volet*]. The condition of salvation is a willing surrender; no one is saved against one's will and desire. However, as he argued in book I about the will, not everyone who wills obtains the happiness they seek. Instead, human willing, afflicted by the penalties of sin ("trouble" and "ignorance"; *FCW* III.18.51), struggles to live rightly and seek the true happiness. But not all power is lost to the will.

However, anyone willing [*voluntatem*] to turn back to God so as to overcome the punishment that his origin deserved in turning away must not only not be hindered but even helped. Thus did the Creator of things show how easily Adam could have remained as he was made, if he had willed [*si voluisset*], since his offspring were able to overcome even what they were born with (*FCW* III.20.55).

Invoking Adam, Augustine addresses the prelapsarian condition of humanity. If only Adam had willed to remain "as he was made" his "offspring" could have been spared the present trouble and ignorance. However, Augustine suggests that such trouble and ignorance can be "overcome" by humanity to reclaim Adam's place. Later on, exploring the origin of the soul, he argues that God implanted in the soul a "natural judgement" [*naturale iudicium*] which makes the soul disposed to seek wisdom and peace: "so that it might attain these things not by being born to them but by pursuing them." However, he then adds that if the soul "is unwilling to do so [*si ... noluerit*], it will be rightly held to be guilty of sin, as a soul which has not used well the ability it received." But then again, he affirms that despite its fallen condition the soul *does* retain the capacity to act. "Although it was born in ignorance and trouble, [the soul] is nevertheless not pressed by any necessity to remain in the condition in which it was born" (*FCW* III.20.56). In fact, as the dialogue proceeds to a conclusion, it is evident that the soul has the capacity to seek truth not based on its *re-creation*, but its original creation. "Therefore, the soul is ignorant of what it ought to do, precisely because it has not yet received it. But it will receive this, too, if it uses well what it *has* received: the power to search diligently and religiously, if it is willing [*si volet*]" (*FCW* III.22.65; translator's emphasis). Again, the qualifying condition "if it is willing." The question to raise is where this willingness originates; this is what Augustine does not do in *Free Choice of the Will*. However, he has put us in position to do so having framed the entire dialogue with the call to "ask, seek, knock" (*FCW* I.16.35; II.2.6; III.20.58), and having invoked the humility of Christ as the way to salvation. "Thus the soul that finds him in outward humility Whom it had forsaken in its inward pride is going to imitate His visible humility and return again to the heights of the invisible" (*FCW* III.10.30).

* * * *

So far, our journey through *Free Choice of the Will* has placed us at the cusp of one of Augustine's major breakthroughs. It has taken us to his discovery of the origin of faith and to the God who has called us and claimed us for himself. "You stir us so that praising you may bring us joy, because you have made us and drawn us to yourself, and our heart is unquiet until it rests in you" (C I.1.1). Or as he puts it a few paragraphs later, "My faith calls upon you, Lord, this faith *which is your gift to me*, which you have breathed into me through the humanity of your Son and the ministry of your preacher" (C I.1.1; emphasis added). The story of how Augustine arrived at this conclusion—that *all* our "possessions," including faith, come from God—is a story many scholars have attempted to tell. Again, though it takes us beyond the remit for this book, the story helpfully frames our conclusions to this Chapter.

Typically, scholars frame the development of Augustine by emphasizing when and how Augustine changed his opinion. After completing three books of *Free Choice of the Will*, they argue, he years later finally declared his approach to be flawed. For, as he confesses retrospectively in *Revisions*, commenting on the question of predestination in Romans 9, "In answering this question I in fact strove on behalf of the free choice of the human will, but God's grace conquered ..." (R II.1.3). Such striving appears evident in *Free Choice of the Will*. Though hampered by obstacles of ignorance and difficulty the soul can, in fact, change course if it assents to. Indeed, we do not need to make a case for this reading but must simply quote Augustine on the change he underwent: "You certainly see what I then held concerning faith and works, though I was working hard to commend the grace of God, and I see that these brothers of ours still hold that view, because they have not taken care to make progress with me as they read my books, as they have taken care to read them." Here, Augustine proposes viewing his change as "progress" and reading his early works as a journey of faith. He therefore repeats: "I worked hard in defense of the free choice of the human will, but the grace of God conquered" (*TPS* 4.8).

Many scholars interpret these statements and others as evidence that Augustine changed his mind about the will (Brown 1967; Fredriksen 1979; Lettieri 2001; Teske 2007). Few indeed would read them as an adequate defense, let alone an excuse covering over his mistakes. Though it may serve Augustine to be read in this way, these scholars suggest, his early works bear witness to a much different author: not a Christian "on the way" to confession of grace (at least inevitably), but a Christian deeply confused over the extent of God's gift. Indeed, as observed in this study already some scholars have extended the implications even further (Dobell 2009). In so doing they offer up a reading of Augustine that encourages deep suspicions of his early intellectual development—even calling into question the validity of his Christian conversion.

Are such suspicions essential to reading the early works? And is it possible to read them in the spirit Augustine urges: a spirit of charity? In response, Augustine could argue that the problem lies with us. We are far too content to look down from the mountain, rather than joining him in the place of security (Chapter 2, Section "Locating Christ in the early works"). Be that as it may, we close this present chapter by referencing the moment he "discovers" God's grace. We will notice that framing his account of God's grace is the command and promise of the one true philosophy—what he believed in all along.

> Who embraces in his heart something that does not attract him? Who has it in his power either to come into contact with what can attract him or to be attracted once he has come into contact? When, therefore, things attract us whereby we may advance towards God, this is inspired and furnished by the grace of God; it is not obtained by our own assent of our will or of our works because, whether it be the assent of our will or our intense effort or our works aglow with charity, it is he who gives, he who bestows it. We are ordered to ask so that we may receive, and to seek so that we may find, and to knock so that it may be opened to us [Mt. 7:7–8]. Is not this particular prayer of ours sometimes so lukewarm, or rather cold and practically non-existent, that we do not notice this in ourselves without sorrow? Because if this actually makes us sorry, we are already praying. What else, then, is being shown to us than that it is he who orders us to ask and to seek and to knock who enables us to do these things? *It is not a matter of willing or of running, but of a merciful God*, since in fact we could neither will nor run if he did not move and rouse us. (*TS* I.2.21)

Conclusion: The Long Surrender

The heart of Augustine's early intellectual development is a journey centered on love and the effect of love's weight. It is a journey not only animated by a restless motive energy, but also haunted by the echo of a voice calling the self: "Where are you?" (Gn. 3:9). Through dialogue, soliloquy, narrative, and prayer, Augustine tried to awaken readers to the reality of love's weight. In that love lies a place unlike any other place, where lovers are disposed to encounter the "Life Questions" that invite them to give an account of themselves: that is, to step forth and make their confession. As Augustine confesses at the end of his *Confessions*, "[M]y weight is my love, and wherever I am carried, it is this weight that carries me."

If my love finds its object in the God who *is* love, then God is not only the source and condition of my weight; God is also the place in which I find eternal rest. Augustine continues.

> Your gift sets us afire and we are borne upward ... By your fire, your beneficent fire, are we enflamed, because we are making our way up *to the peace of Jerusalem.* For *I rejoiced when I was told,* "We are going to the Lord's house" [Ps. 121:6,1]. There shall a good will [*bona voluntate*] find us a place, that we may have no other desire but to abide there forever. (*C* XIII.9.10)

Here, the goodwill is invoked once again, only this time clearly grounded and unfolded by God's gift. It is clear that this place is where Augustine wants to be, and also where he wants all his readers to arrive at.

In the prologue to book IV of his famous *The Trinity*, he describes the kind of lover he desires to engage. Many seek knowledge of "earthly and celestial things" yet without also reflecting on their own "health and strength." "But take a man," he writes, "who has been roused [*excitatus*] by the warmth of the Holy Spirit and has already woken up [*evigilavit*] to God"—this man does not dally on the road to salvation. Instead, "in loving [God] he has become cheap [*viluit*] in his own estimation"—that is, he has become like Christ who became "cheap" (cf. *HGJ* 1.8, 13). Moreover, in "being eager yet unable to go in to [God], he has taken a look at himself in God's light, and discovered himself, and realized that his own sickness cannot be compounded with God's cleanness." Now occupying the place of confession, prayer, and weeping—the place of the moral self—this man starts to reclaim himself as a lover.

> Well, such a man, poor and grieving in this way, is not *puffed up* by *knowledge* because he is *built up* by *charity* (1 Cor. 8:1), since he has valued knowledge above knowledge; he has put knowledge of his own weakness above knowledge of the *walls of the world*, the foundations of the earth and the pinnacles of the sky; and by *bringing in* this *knowledge* he has *brought in sorrow* (Eccl. 1:18), the sorrow of the exile stirred by longing for his true country and its founder, his blissful God.

Not surprisingly, Augustine adds in the following line that he too occupies this place of confession: "As one of this sort of men, O Lord my God, I sigh among your poor ones in the family of your Christ ..." (*TT* IV.1.1).

For Augustine, confession is a form of self-knowing that relinquishes control over the place of the self. It is not, however, a total self-surrender, but paradoxically gives the self *back* to itself in truth. By "in truth," we mean God holds the place of the self. God does not abandon his creation to its fate. Instead, calling it back to its place before him, God reveals the truth of the way things are, including the moral realities that confront and engage us. On our reading, Augustine's journey is a continuous unfolding of the many sundry ways God remains where we are, "more intimately present to me than my innermost being ..." (*C* III.6.11). In this way, self-knowledge is not an end in itself but unfolds in the infinite mystery and otherness of God.

CONCLUSION: THE LONG SURRENDER

Moreover, precisely because it is a place of confession, the moral self does not cease to take part in the world, even though Augustine was once tempted to do so. Confession is the way one *navigates* the world, attending to the call echoing across the moral landscape. One hears that call in the mundane and the extraordinary, in a landscape ever-shifting, difficult to map, and full of distraction. It is there in the experience of ourselves as moral agents: in the moment we are summoned to be where we are and in the moment we accept or decline that summons. In this light, the accusation often lodged against Augustine—that he is too "otherworldly" and not attentive to embodied reality—has a tendency to ignore how God's call animates the self. There are events that ground us, encounters that command us, but none is sufficient to give an account of the self. Part of why they cannot provide this account is that they pose *without resolving* the haunting questions of existence. To experience the world without these questions in view—to ignore them, suppress them, even deny them altogether—is to entertain the atomization and dissolution of the self. Indeed, it is to attack the very idea of human community, denying this community any place in the world. As Oliver O'Donovan contends,

> It is possible to refuse the mighty answers of the Reformed catechism, "Man's chief and highest end is to glorify God, and fully to enjoy him for ever," because creation *is* contingent and man's place in it *can* be understood solely in terms of his "natural" rather than his "supernatural" end. But it is not possible for humanism to refuse the *question*, "What is the chief and highest end of man?" For without some answer to that question it has lost, not only the grounds for respecting this human species (thus leaving itself engaged upon a pointless self-worship), but also ... the very reason to understand humanity as a unitary species at all, rather than as a chance objectification, or "tragic thrownness," of being. (O'Donovan 1994: 38)

In the place of the moral self one learns to confess, acknowledging the weight of love bearing the self up to God. In this act, one discovers oneself among others and receives from others (and the Other) validation of one's place: we are "on the way" to the peace of Jerusalem, the city on a hill that we abide in through faith. With this knowledge, one gradually begins to perceive *this* reality as also taking part in the story of salvation. Creation, now revealed as the "delight of the Lord" (*EP* 26[2]), becomes a place full of enchantment and mysterious purpose. Augustine's advice to those people on the way is to look up: not turning away from the goodness of creation, but in the sense of taking part in the *same source* of goodness (*EP* 26[2].8). In this way, he teaches them to dwell in creation by loving what enfolds all of creation into itself.

In the last analysis, the abiding invitation of Augustine's legacy is to reclaim by surrendering to the place of confession. The question "Where are you?" lives on in our age, for it is a question not based on human being, knowing, willing. It comes to us in love, and is received by us through love, for love is the beginning and the end of our journey. "Give me a lover, and he will know by experience what I am saying here. Give me a man of desires, give me someone who is traveling thirsty through this wilderness, and panting for the fountain of eternal life, and he will know what I am saying" (*HGJ* 26.4). In an age that calls us into question all the time, having taken so much from our humanity already, Augustine suggests that there is a question that holds us in place; come down, then, he says, and find rest for your souls.

REFERENCES

Arendt, Hannah (1971), *The Life of the Mind: One/Thinking: Two/Willing*, San Diego, CA: Harcourt.
Arendt, Hannah (1996), *Love and Saint Augustine*, eds. J. Vecchiarelli Scott and J. Chelius Stark, Chicago: The University of Chicago Press.
Babcock, William (1988), "Augustine on Sin and Moral Agency," *Journal of Religious Ethics* 16, 38, 39.
Babcock, William, ed. (1991), *The Ethics of St. Augustine*, Atlanta, GA: Scholar's Press.
Bartholomew, Craig G. (2011), *Where Mortals Dwell: A Christian View of Place for Today*, Grand Rapids, MI: Baker Academic.
Boone, Mark J. (2016), *The Conversion and Therapy of Desire: Augustine's Theology of Desire in the Cassiciacum Dialogues*, Eugene, OR: Wipf and Stock.
Brittain, Charles (2006), *Cicero: On Academic Scepticism*, Indianapolis, IN: Hackett, viii–iviii.
Brown, Peter (2000 [1967]), *Augustine of Hippo: A Biography*, 2nd ed., Berkeley, CA: University of California Press.
Brown, Robert (1978), "The First Evil Will Must Be Incomprehensible: A Critique of Augustine," *Journal of the American Academy of Religion* 46.3, 315.
Bruner, Jerome (2000), *Making Stories: Law, Literature, Life*, Cambridge, MA: Harvard University Press.
Burnaby, John (1939), *Amor Dei: A Study of the Religion of St. Augustine*, Norwich: The Canterbury Press.
Burnell, Peter (2005), *The Augustinian Person*, Washington, DC: The Catholic University of America Press.
Byers, Sarah, "The Meaning of *Voluntas* in Augustine," *Augustinian Studies* 37.2, 171–189.
Cameron, Michael (2012), *Christ Meets Me Everywhere: Augustine's Early Figurative Exegesis*, Oxford: Oxford University Press.
Canning, Raymond (1993), *The Unity of the Love for God and Neighbour in St. Augustine*, Heverlee-Leuven: Augustinian Historical Institute.
Cary, Philip (1996), "Believing the Word: A Proposal about Knowing Other Persons," *Faith & Philosophy* 13.1, 78–90.

Cary, Philip (1999), "Interiority," *Augustine through the Ages*, ed. Allan D. Fitzgerald, O.S.A., Grand Rapids, MI: William B. Eerdmans, 454–456.
Cary, Philip (2000), *Augustine's Invention of the Inner Self: The Legacy of a Christian Platonist*, Oxford: Oxford University Press.
Cary, Philip (2008a), *Inner Grace: Augustine in the Traditions of Plato and Paul*, Oxford: Oxford University Press.
Cary, Philip (2008b), *Outward Signs: The Powerlessness of External Things in Augustine's Thought*, Oxford: Oxford University Press.
Casey, Edward S. (1998), *The Fate of Place: A Philosophical History*, Los Angeles: University of California Press.
Catapano, Giovanni (2006), "Quale scetticismo viene criticato da Agostino nel *Contra Academicos*?," *Quaestio* 6, 1–13.
Cavadini, John C. (2007), "The Darkest Enigma: Reconsidering the Self in Augustine's Thought," *Augustinian Studies* 38.1, 119–132.
Connolly, William (2002), *The Augustinian Imperative: Reflections on the Politics of Morality*, new ed., Lanham, MD: Rowman & Littlefield.
Conybeare, Catherine (2005), "The Duty of a Teacher: Liminality and *disciplina* in Augustine's *De ordine*," *Augustine and the Disciplines: From Cassiciacum to Confessions*, eds. Karla Pollmann and Mark Vessey, Oxford: Oxford University Press, 45–65.
Conybeare, Catherine (2006), *The Irrational Augustine*, Oxford: Oxford University Press.
Curley, Augustine J. (1997), *Augustine's Critique of Skepticism: A Study of "Contra Academicos,"* New York: Peter Lang.
Dewart, Joanna McWilliam (1984), "Augustine's Developing Use of the Cross: 387–400," *Augustinian Studies* 15, 15–33.
Dihle, Albrecht (1982), *The Theory of Will in Classical Antiquity*, Berkeley, CA: University of California Press.
Djuth, Marianne (2007), "Philosophy in a Time of Exile: Vera Philosophia and the Incarnation," *Augustinian Studies* 38.1, 281–300.
Dobell, Brian (2009), *Augustine's Intellectual Conversion: The Journey from Platonism to Christianity*, Cambridge: Cambridge University Press.
Douglass, Laurie (1996), "Voice Recast: Augustine's Use of Conversion in *De ordine* and the *Confessions*," *Augustinian Studies* 27.1, 39–54.
Drever, Matthew (2013), *Image, Identity, and the Forming of the Augustinian Soul*, Oxford: Oxford University Press.
DuPont, Anthony (2008), "Continuity or Discontinuity in Augustine?," *Ars Disputandi* 8.1, 69–81.
Evans, G.R. (1990), *Augustine on Evil*, Cambridge: Cambridge University Press.
Fitzgerald, Allan D. OSA (2014), "Christ's Humility and Christian Humility in the *De Civitate Dei*," *Mayéutica* 40, 241–261.

Foley, Michael P. (1999), "Cicero, Augustine, and the Philosophical Roots of the Cassiciacum Dialogues," *Revue des Études Augustiniènnes* 45, 51–77.
Fortin, Charles (1970), "The Political Implications of St. Augustine's Theory of Conscience," *Augustinian Studies* 1, 133–152.
Fredriksen, Paula (1979), "Augustine's Early Interpretation of Paul," Ph.D. Dissertation: Princeton University.
Gerber, Chad Tyler (2012), *The Spirit of Augustine's Early Theology: Contextualizing Augustine's Pneumatology*, Surrey: Ashgate.
Gilson, Étienne (1960), *The Christian Philosophy of Saint Augustine*, tr. L.E.M. Lynch, London: Lowe & Brydon.
Gilson, Étienne (2009 [1971]), *From Aristotle to Darwin and Back Again: A Journey in Final Causality, Species, and Evolution*, tr. John Lyon, San Francisco, CA: Ignatius Press.
Gregory, Brad S. (2012), *The Unintended Reformation: How a Religious Revolution Secularized Society*, Cambridge, MA and London: Harvard University Press.
Gregory, Eric (2008), *Politics and the Order of Love: An Augustinian Ethic of Democratic Citizenship*, Chicago: University of Chicago Press.
Hadot, Pierre (1995), *Philosophy as a Way of Life: From Socrates to Foucault*, London: Blackwell.
Hanby, Michael (2003), *Augustine and Modernity*, London: Routledge.
Harding, Brian (2003), "Skepticism, Illumination and Christianity in Augustine's *Contra Academicos*," *Augustinian Studies* 34.2, 197–212.
Harding, Brian (2006), "Epistemology and Eudaimonism in Augustine's *Contra Academicos*," *Augustinian Studies* 37.2, 247–271.
Harding, Brian (2008), *Augustine and Roman Virtue*, London: Continuum.
Harrison, Carol (1992), *Beauty and Revelation in the thought of Saint Augustine*, Oxford: Clarendon Press.
Harrison, Carol (2000), *Augustine: Christian Truth and Fractured Humanity*, Oxford: Oxford University Press.
Harrison, Carol (2006), *Rethinking Augustine's Early Theology: An Argument for Continuity*, Oxford: Oxford University Press.
Harrison, Simon (1999), "Autobiographical Identity and Philosophical Past in Augustine's Dialogue *De libero arbitrio*," *Constructing Identities in Late Antiquity*, ed. R. Miles, London: Routledge.
Harrison, Simon (2006), *Augustine's Way into the Will: The Theological and Philosophical Significance of "De libero arbitrio,"* Oxford: Oxford University Press.
Hart, David Bentley (2003), "Christ and Nothing," *First Things* (October), 47–56.

Hauerwas, Stanley (1972), "Love's Not All You Need," *Cross Currents* 32, 225–237.
Heschel, Abraham (2007 [1955]), *God in Search of Man: A Philosophy of Judaism*, London: Souvenir's Press.
Holte, Ragnar (1962), *Béatitude et sagesse: Saint Augustin et le problèm de la fin de l'homme dans la philosophie anciene*, Paris: Études Augustiniennes.
Holte, Ragnar (1994), "Monnica, 'the Philosopher,'" *Augustinus* 39, 293–316.
Irwin, T.H. (1992), "Who Discovered the Will?," *Philosophical Perspectives: Ethics* 6, 453–573.
Kahn, Charles H. (1988), "Discovering the Will: From Aristotle to Augustine," *The Question of Eclecticism: Studies in Later Greek Philosophy*, eds. J.M. Dillon and A.A. Long, Berkeley, CA: University of California Press, 234–259.
Kierkegaard, Søren (2009 [1962]), *Works of Love*, tr. Howard and Edna Hong, New York: HarperCollins.
Kirwan, Christopher (1989), *Augustine*, London: Duckworth.
Kolbet, Paul R. (2009), *Augustine and the Cure of Souls: Revising a Classical Ideal*, South Bend, IN: Notre Dame University Press.
Lee, Kam-Lun Edwin (1999), *Augustine, Manichaeism, and the Good*. Patristic Studies 2, New York: Peter Lang.
Lettieri, Gaetano (2001), *L'altro Agostino. Ermeneutica e retorica della grazia dalla crisi alla metamorfosi del* De doctrina christiana, Ed. Morcelliana, Brescia.
Lieu, Samuel N.C. (1985), *Manichaeism in the Later Roman Empire and Medieval China: A Historical Survey*, Manchester: Manchester University Press.
MacIntyre, Alasdair (2006), *The Tasks of Philosophy: Selected Essays, Vol. 1*, Cambridge: Cambridge University Press.
Madec, Goulven (1996), *Introduction aux "Révisions" et à la lecture des oeuvres de saint Augustin*, Collection des Études Augustiniennes, Série Antiquité 150, Paris: Institute d'Études Augustiniennes.
Manent, Pierre (2013), *Metamorphoses of the City: On the Western Dynamic*, Cambridge, MA: Cambridge University Press.
Marion, Jean-Luc (2007), *The Erotic Phenomenon*, tr. Stephen E. Lewis, Chicago: University of Chicago Press.
Marion, Jean-Luc (2012), *In the Self's Place: The Approach of Augustine*, tr. Jeffrey L. Kosky, Standford, CA: Stanford University Press.
Mathewes, Charles T. (1999), "Augustinian Anthropology: Intimo Interior Meo," *Journal of Religious Ethics* 27.2, 195–221.
May, Simon (2011), *Love: A History*, New Haven, CT: Yale University Press.
McWilliam, Joanne (1990), "The Cassiciacum Autobiography," *Studia Patristica* 18.4, 14–43.

Nietzsche, Friedrich (2006 [1882]), *The Gay Science*, tr. Thomas Common, Mineola, New York: Dover.

Nussbaum, Martha (1990), *Love's Knowledge: Essays on Philosophy and Literature*, New York and Oxford: Oxford University Press.

Nussbaum, Martha (2009), *The Therapy of Desire: Theory and Practice in Hellenistic Ethics*, Princeton, NJ: Princeton University Press.

Obdrzalek, Suzanne (2006), "Living in Doubt: Carneades' *Pithanon* Reconsidered," *Oxford Studies in Ancient Philosophy* 31, 243–279.

O'Connell, Robert J. (1968), *St. Augustine's Early Theory of Man, A.D. 386–391*, Cambridge, MA: Harvard University Press.

O'Connell, Robert J. (1970), "*De libero arbitrio* I: Stoicism Revisited," *Augustinian Studies* 1, 49–68.

O'Connell, Robert J. (1986), "On Augustine's First Conversion: Factus Erectior (De Beata Vita 4)," *Augustinian Studies* 17, 15–29.

O'Connell, Robert J. (1994), "The Visage of Philosophy at Cassiciacum," *Augustinian Studies* 25.

O'Connell, Robert J. (1996), *Images of Conversion in St. Augustine's Confessions*, New York: Fordham University Press.

O'Daly, Gerard (2001), "The Response to Skepticism and the Mechanics of Cognition," *Cambridge Companion to Augustine*, eds. Eleonore Stump and Norman Kretzmann, Cambridge: Cambridge University Press, 159–170.

O'Donovan, Oliver (1980), *The Problem of Self-Love in St. Augustine*, New Haven, CT: Yale University Press.

O'Donovan, Oliver (1982), "*Usus* and *Fruitio* in Augustine, *De Doctrina Christiana* 1," *Journal of Theological Studies* 33.2, 361–397.

O'Donovan, Oliver (1994), *Resurrection and Moral Order: An Outline for Evangelical Ethics*, 2nd ed., Grand Rapids, MI: William B. Eerdmans.

O'Donovan, Oliver (2002), *Common Objects of Love: The Moral Shaping of Community*, Grand Rapids, MI: William B. Eerdmans.

O'Donovan, Oliver (2005), *The Ways of Judgment*, Grand Rapids, MI: William B. Eerdmans.

O'Donovan, Oliver (2013), *Self, World, and Time: Ethics as Theology, An Induction*, vol. 1, Grand Rapids, MI: William B. Eerdmans.

O'Donovan, Oliver (2014), *Finding and Seeking: Ethics as Theology*, vol. 2, Grand Rapids, MI: William B. Eerdmans.

O'Donovan, Oliver (2015), "Know Thyself! The Return of Self-Love," *The Authority of the Gospel: Explorations in Moral and Political Theology in Honor of Oliver O'Donovan*, eds. Robert Song and Brent Waters, Grand Rapids, MI: William B. Eerdmans.

Patterson, James F. (2016), "Augustine's Fig Tree (Confessiones 8.12.28)," *Augustinian Studies* 47.2, 181–200.

Pollmann, Karla et al., eds. (2013), *The Oxford Guide to the Historical Reception of Augustine*, 3 vols., Oxford: Oxford University Press.

Power, Kim (1996), *Veiled Desire: Augustine on Women*, New York: Continuum.
Rist, John M. (1994), *Augustine: Ancient Thought Baptized*, Cambridge: Cambridge University Press.
Rist, John M. (2001), "Faith and Reason," *Cambridge Companion to Augustine*, eds. Eleonore Stump and Norman Kretzmann, Cambridge: Cambridge University Press, 26–39.
Rist, John M. (2014), *Augustine Deformed: Love, Sin and Freedom in the Western Moral Tradition*, Cambridge: Cambridge University Press.
Scruton, Roger (2012), *The Soul of the World*, Princeton, NJ: Princeton University Press.
Siedentop, Larry (2014), *Inventing the Individual: The Origins of Modern Liberalism*, Cambridge, MA: Harvard University Press.
Smith, James K.A. (2016), *You Are What You Love: The Spiritual Power of Habit*, Grand Rapids, MI: Brazos Press.
Sorabji, Richard (2014), *Moral Conscience through the Ages: Fifth Century BCE to the Present*, Chicago: University of Chicago Press.
Stock, Brian (1996), *Augustine the Reader: Meditation, Self-Knowledge, and the Ethics of Interpretation*, Cambridge, MA: Harvard University Press.
Stock, Brian (2010), *Augustine's Inner Dialogue: The Philosophical Soliloquy in Late Antiquity*, Cambridge: Cambridge University Press.
Svensson, Manfred (2013), "Augustine on Moral Conscience," *The Heythrop Journal* 54, 43–54.
Taylor, Charles (1989), *Sources of the Self: The Making of the Modern Identity*, Cambridge: Cambridge University Press.
Taylor, Charles (2007), *A Secular Age*, Cambridge, MA: Harvard University Press.
Teske, S.J. Roland (2007), "Augustine's Third Conversion: A Case for Discontinuity," *Proceedings of the Jesuit Philosophical Association*, ed. Joseph Koterski, 19–38.
Testard, Maurice (1958), *Saint Augustin et Cicéron*, 2 vol., *Repertoire des textes*, Paris: Études Augustiniennes.
Thorsrud, Harald (2009), *Ancient Scepticism*, Stocksfield: Acumen.
Topping, Ryan N.S. (2012), *Happiness and Wisdom: Augustine's Early Theology of Education*, Washington DC: The Catholic University of America Press.
Torchia, N. Joseph (1990), "*Pondus Meum Amor Meus:* The Weight-Metaphor in St. Augustine's Early Philosophy," *Augustinian Studies* 21, 163–176.
Tracy, David (2008), "Augustine's Christomorphic Theocentrism," *Orthodox Readings of Augustine*, eds. Aristotle Papanikolaou and George E. Demacopoulos, Crestwood, NY: St. Vladimir's Seminary Press.

Turner, Denys (1995), *The Darkness of God: Negativity in Christian Mysticism*, Cambridge: Cambridge University Press.
Ward, Graham (2005), *Christ and Culture*, Oxford: Blackwell.
Weil, Simone (2003), "To Desire without an Object," *Gravity and Grace*, tr. Emma Crawford and Mario von der Ruhr, London and New York: Routledge.
Wetzel, James (1992), *Augustine and the Limits of Virtue*, Cambridge: Cambridge University Press.
Williams, Rowan (2003), *Christ on Trial: How the Gospel Unsettles Our Judgment*, Grand Rapids, MI: William B. Eerdmans.
Yeats, W.B. (1994 [1919]), "The Second Coming," *The Collected Poems of W.B. Yeats*, 158–159.

INDEX

Academics (Skeptics) 47–9
Adam, in Genesis 31–43, 59–60, 74–6, 81, 88–90, 96, 102, 118–21
Ambrose, St. 37, 51, 55, 67, 104–5
Augustine, writings of
   The Academics 12, 27–8, 45, 47–71, 79, 91, 116
   The Advantage of Believing 76–7
   The Catholic and Manichean Ways of Life 11, 27, 76–80, 83–5, 90, 92–3, 96–7, 110, 118
   Confessions 1–3, 17–23, 26–7, 34, 37–45, 50–1, 54–5, 58, 82, 85, 103–5, 118–19, 125
   Expositions of the Psalms 11, 25, 27–8, 85–6, 99, 110, 128
   Free Choice of the Will 101–23
   Genesis: A Refutation of the Manichees 33–7, 59, 64, 76, 94, 98
   The Happy Life 45, 52–3, 58–9, 67, 113
   On Order 56, 67, 87, 91, 95–6
   Revisions 71, 122
   The Soliloquies 91
   True Religion 43, 54, 73–99, 113
authority 75–85, 89, 94, 110. See also Christ
   of conscience 36
   of philosophers 47, 56, 59

autobiography (first-personal perspective) 17, 20, 41, 108
awakening 15, 27, 43, 48–52, 59, 66–7, 71, 113

beauty 21, 88, 92
being, knowing, willing (*esse, nosse, vivere*) 7, 9, 11, 14–16, 25, 58, 87, 97, 128
Bible (Scripture) 20, 34, 40, 50, 84, 103
   Gn. 3:9, 11, 29, 31, 33, 84, 102, 125, 128
   Matt. 7:7, 13, 27, 29, 31, 46, 49, 53, 55, 60, 63, 73, 77, 85, 95, 98, 121
   Ps. 4, 50–1, 63, 68, 70, 85–6, 89, 93, 110
body 28, 59, 71, 79–80, 88–9, 94–7
"books of the Platonists" 41, 53, 103–4, 114, 119
Brown, P. 102, 122
Burnaby, J. 27–8

Cameron, M. 34, 43, 81, 84
Carneades 61, 66, 71
Cary, P. 6, 52, 87, 90–1, 118
Cassiciacum 45, 48–9, 53, 78
Cavadini, J.C. 8–11
Christ 31, 41–6, 81–5
   authority of 40, 48, 64, 71, 78, 85
   as discipline 91, 94–5

138 INDEX

as example 79–84
as Form/Word 42–4, 83–4, 86–7, 93–5
and salvation 43–4, 81–3
and true philosophy 42–3, 46, 91
as Truth 37, 43, 77, 87, 91–2, 110, 118
as Virtue and Wisdom of God 43, 64, 82–3, 118
Cicero, M.T. 27, 52–3, 56–64, 69–70, 78, 108
  Academica 61–2
  Hortensius 53, 59–60, 108
cogito, Augustinian 112–16
confession
  aim of 21–2, 27, 39, 40, 94–5, 103
  humility of 43–4, 70, 98, 123
  place of 27, 35, 38, 73, 79, 97–9, 103, 125–8
conscience 31, 36–40, 98–9, 104, 109–11, 118–20
contemplation 85, 93
conversion, Augustine's 38–46
Conybeare, C. 48–9, 66
Courcelle, P. 59
creation 59, 88–9, 92–9, 104–8, 112–21, 126–8
curiosity (*curiositas*) 93–4

delight 28, 45, 76, 99, 113, 117, 118, 128
desire. *See also* happy life; love; truth
  for home 3–4, 21–6, 40, 45, 71, 89, 99
  journey of 2, 27, 31, 45, 76, 92, 96, 125–8
  in modernity 7–11
  as sin 21, 26–9, 33–4, 37, 81, 111, 114, 118
  to be like God 24, 33–8, 75, 90, 94

despair (*desperatio veri*) 28, 49, 53–4, 57, 63, 65, 70, 74–5, 79, 114, 116–17
dialectic 41, 48, 61–2, 91
dialogue
  inner (soliloquy) 14, 87–92
  use of 14, 48, 51, 55, 58, 116
Dihle, A. 102
divinity of soul 51–2, 90, 104
Dobell, B. 14, 43–4, 81–2, 123

early works, Augustine's 12–14
Eden, garden of 33, 38–9
embodiment 89, 127
eternal life 113, 128
evil
  blaming God for 35, 102, 105–9, 114
  Manichean conception of 103–5
  origin of 103–8, 110–11, 118–19
  as privation 103, 119–20
  problem of 40, 103, 111–14, 119
exercise of the mind 1, 65, 77, 87, 101
external (outer, outside) world 6, 91–2, 97–8

faith 63, 65–70, 77, 84, 102–11, 115, 120, 122
Foley, M.P. 53, 61

Gerber, C.T. 14, 51, 83, 93, 95
Gilson, E. 2, 6
Good
  in creation 21–2, 74–6, 88–9, 99, 128
  God is 75, 86, 99, 103, 104–8, 114, 118–20
  highest (*summum bonum*) 71, 79–80, 117–18
grace 32, 77, 85, 98, 122–3

INDEX

Hadot, P. 27
happy life, desire for 45–6, 51–2, 54–8, 79–80, 87, 113, 116–18
Harding, B. 27, 49, 58, 62–3
Harrison, C. 14, 41, 88–9, 102
Harrison, S. 102, 105, 108–10, 112, 115–16
human nature 81, 84, 97, 112

ignorance 62, 66, 104, 120–2
illumination (enlightenment) 49, 74–5, 104
image of God 33, 55, 59, 83–90, 93–5, 110, 118
"in," meaning of 86–92
intellect (mind) 65, 71, 75, 78, 80, 87, 89, 91–2, 114, 119
interiority (inner self/man) 10, 19–21, 85–7, 91–2, 95–6, 126

Kant, I. 117
Kierkegaard, S. 5
Kirwan, C. 57–8

law
  eternal 95, 110–11, 118
  temporal 110–11
liberal arts 91
"Life Questions" 29, 125
love. *See also* desire; philosophy
  ambiguity of 25
  as center of moral life 1, 6–7, 15
  definition of 16–17, 25
  double command to 83, 96–8
  in relation to reason 16
  weight of 1, 7, 11, 15–16, 27, 57–8, 87, 96, 125–7

Madec, G. 102
Manichees (Manichaeism)
  in Genesis 75–6
  materialism 103–5, 110, 119
  rationalism 78, 89
  and seeking 33–6, 50, 53–4, 60, 73–4, 76–81, 84–5, 101
Marion, J.-L. 20, 29, 79
May, S. 17, 24–6
modernity 2–9, 24–6
Monica 16–21, 54, 66–7
moral self
  definition of 2, 8–12, 112
  and love 7, 15–16, 70
  place of 11, 27, 35, 44, 63–4, 70, 92, 96–7, 101–2, 126–7

Nietzsche, F. 4, 24
nothingness (the void) 4, 49, 54

O'Connell, R.J. 18, 28, 42, 59–60, 64
O'Donovan, O. 7, 16, 40, 78, 83, 89
order. *See also* providence; "the way things are"
  of human beings 109–10, 112–15, 118
  of love 7–9, 35, 37, 85, 99, 110, 112–15, 118
otherness 2, 6, 10–12, 16–21, 22, 32, 42, 91–2, 96–8, 126–7

Paul, St. 60, 86, 93
Pelagius 102
philosophy. *See also* Christ
  and Christianity 42–6, 48–9, 64, 66–7, 109
  as love of wisdom 25–9, 53, 55–6, 59–60, 63
  obstacles to life of 28–9, 53–4, 65, 69, 106, 122
Plato 47, 64, 108
Platonists 41–5, 52, 66, 107, 114
Plotinus 52–3
prayer 20, 55, 63–71, 95, 99, 123, 125–6

pride (*superbia*) 31, 33–7, 45–6,
    55, 75–6, 81, 90, 121
  in Manichaeism 21, 53–4,
    73–6, 79
  in skepticism 45, 53–5, 65, 69
providence 51, 55, 60, 74, 77–9,
    80, 85, 87, 98, 106, 109
purification 22

reading books 52–3, 59–60, 84
reason 15–16, 40, 45, 51, 75,
    77–81, 104, 110–14
  as standing upright (*factus
    erectior*) 59–60, 84–5,
    87–97
restless heart 1, 12, 15, 22, 26–7,
    55, 125
resurrection 81–2
Rist, J.M. 3, 27, 29, 77, 108, 109,
    112
Romanianus, Augustine's patron
    49–55, 63–5, 68, 73–4,
    76–7

Scripture. *See* Bible
senses 89, 94
sin. *See* curiosity; desire; evil; pride
skepticism (New Academy). *See
    also* Carneades; Cicero
  hidden legacy of 47–9, 64, 71
  persuasive impressions (*to
    pithanon*) 61
  suspension of assent (*epochē*)
    48, 61–3, 68–71
soliloquy. *See* dialogue
soul
  nature of 35–6, 51–2, 75–6,
    79–81, 86, 90–1, 94–5
  needs of 22–5, 84–5, 98

origin of 18, 109, 115, 121
reformation of 83–4, 87–8,
    93–5, 110
turn to 85–92, 94–5
Stock, B. 14, 52, 84, 87, 102, 108,
    110
Stoicism 47, 61, 117
surrender, posture of 1–2, 11,
    13–14, 38, 126
  against Manichaeism 73–4, 94,
    110, 120
  against skepticism 64, 69–71,
    73–4

Taylor, C. 5–6
Teske, R. 83, 122
Testard, M. 45
Theology, Christian 27, 29, 109
"the way things are" (*ordo rerum*)
    31, 35, 36, 58, 74–5, 84, 92,
    95, 126
Thorsrud, H. 61–3
Topping, R.N.S. 14, 41, 58, 77,
    102
Trinity, doctrine of 67, 83, 92–3
truth, desire for 34, 37, 54–8, 63,
    115–17

virtue 34, 66–7, 70, 80, 83–4, 98,
    114. *See also* Christ
voluntarism 15, 112

Wetzel, J. 80, 102, 114
will or willing (*voluntas*)
  definition of 112
  good will 70, 75, 78–9, 84, 95,
    117–18, 125
wisdom, definition of 63
wise man (*sapiens*) 61, 67–70, 82

www.ingramcontent.com/pod-product-compliance
Lightning Source LLC
Chambersburg PA
CBHW070338240426
43665CB00045B/2225